estherpress

Books for Courageous Women

ESTHER PRESS VISION

Publishing diverse voices that encourage and equip women to walk courageously in the light of God's truth for such a time as this.

BIBLICAL STATEMENT OF PURPOSE

"For if you keep silent at this time, relief and deliverance will rise for the Jews from another place, but you and your father's house will perish. And who knows whether you have not come to the kingdom for such a time as this?"

Esther 4:14 (ESV)

What people are saying about …

She Belongs

"We all want to belong. We want to feel loved and seen. The beauty of the gospel is that God invites each of us into a safe and sacred space of community through Jesus. This Bible study by Katy McCown will lead you on a powerful and personal journey of feeling, healing, and hope as each story, study question, prayer, and passage of Scripture points to the many ways you're uniquely designed to live out—and live in—the love of God and His people."

Gwen Smith, host of the *Graceologie* podcast, speaker, coach, author of *I Want It All*

"I meet women every day who have a deep desire to belong to a safe and loving community. Most believe they are the only one who feels lost and alone in this world. What Katy McCown has written in this study will minister to women of all ages and walks of life by pointing them to a God who is earnestly looking for them. Her use of story and guided Bible study will encourage every heart to first connect with the Father and then with like-minded sisters. Belonging can be beautiful, and this study is a perfect place to start."

Stacey Thacker, speaker, author of *Threadbare Prayer*, women's ministry director at First Baptist Orlando

"If you've ever felt like there isn't a place for you in the church, this study is for you! Through her own stories, full of honesty and tenderness, Katy McCown gently leads us through the Word to the beautiful truth of belonging that we find in Jesus—and in His church."

Ann Swindell, author of *The Path to Peace* and owner of Writing with Grace

"I know that empty feeling to desire to belong, or to be accepted by others. I also know how hard it is to encourage and guide others who are seeking those same desires but feel as though they will never reach that place. Sisters, you are not alone. Using Scripture and life experiences, Katy reminds us of what we must do to be full and belong in Christ. She strategically guides with thought-provoking questions to evaluate everyone's individual walk with Christ while encouraging them to seek a community where they can worship and grow together in Christ. Whether you are a young woman, a new Christian, or a seasoned Christian leader, this study is a great tool to bring all women together for the purpose of cultivating growth and belonging with other sisters in Christ."

Terri Orr, women's ministry director, Cornerstone Baptist Church

"Often we are tempted to think that we can follow Jesus without being rooted and connected in his bride, the church. Individual salvation only exists so God can have a family. This beautiful multiethnic family is called the body of Christ. In *She Belongs*, Katy has written a compelling Bible study that will enrich the lives of all who read it."

Derwin L. Gray, cofounder and lead pastor of Transformation Church, author of *How to Heal Our Racial Divide*

She
Belongs

AN INTERACTIVE
BIBLE STUDY

Includes Six-Session
Video Series

KATY MCCOWN

She Belongs

Finding Your
Place in the Body of Christ

estherpress

Books for Courageous Women
from David C Cook

SHE BELONGS
Published by Esther Press,
an imprint of David C Cook
4050 Lee Vance Drive
Colorado Springs, CO 80918 U.S.A.

Integrity Music Limited, a division of David C Cook
Brighton, East Sussex BN1 2RE, England

ISBN 978-0-8307-8462-2
eISBN 978-0-8307-8463-9

The author is represented by and this book is published in association with the literary
agency of WordServe Literary Group, Ltd., www.wordserveliterary.com.

The Team: Susan McPherson, Jeff Gerke, Judy Gillispie, James Hershberger, Susan Murdock
Cover Design: Emily Weigel

Printed in the United States of America
First Edition 2023

1 2 3 4 5 6 7 8 9 10

041423

To Nanna,

for always taking Mom to church and
always taking me to church,
for your beautiful soprano voice that I still
try to replicate most Sunday mornings.

Until we worship Jesus together again in heaven.

Meet the Author

Katy McCown is the author of *She Smiles without Fear: Proverbs 31 for Every Woman*, a writer for Proverbs 31 Ministries, and a national speaker. Katy's Bible-teaching days began in her home as a young adult. From the floor of her children's bedroom to the living room where she gathered with other women, Katy has spent more than a decade opening God's Word and teaching it to others. In 2017, Katy joined the First 5 team at Proverbs 31 Ministries, where she continues to study, train, and teach the Bible.

Katy is married to former NFL quarterback Luke McCown. She left her job as a television news reporter to join him on his adventure in the National Football League. During his thirteen years in the NFL, they moved more than a dozen times as Luke played on six teams, primarily as a backup quarterback. Through all the uncertainties and surprises, Katy has learned some things about "living sure" even when the future is not, because even when God's path seemed to sideline her plans, it never sidelined her purpose.

Luke and Katy have six children, plus a dog and a cat who take turns bothering each other. Katy loves a cup of strong coffee—or two—and her van is never clean. Never ever.

Connect with Katy at www.katymccown.com, or follow her on Instagram and Facebook.

Katy @SheLaughsConference.Com

He makes the whole body fit together perfectly. As each part does its own special work, it helps the other parts grow, so that the whole body is healthy and growing and full of love.

Ephesians 4:16 NLT

Contents

Week 4: Living Your Most Complete Life

Week 5: What Happens When We Belong

Introduction

I've Got This

I squinted and tried not to look directly at the sun glaring down on me. As I averted my attention to anything else, the sun seemed to bounce off the snow that surrounded me. I wondered how long I would lie there.

Surely, I thought, *someone will come by and help me.* As one person after another passed without a word, my hopes shifted from someone stopping to help me to someone at least telling another person I needed help … and then maybe *that* person would come to my rescue.

It was my own fault. I had most definitely gotten myself into this mess, and now I had to rely on someone—anyone—to help me out of it. *It* was a mountain. A steep mountain. That I had attempted to ski down all by myself.

I hadn't begun my journey alone. I had reached the top of the mountain with my mom and my sister. As we exited the ski lift and they paused to wait on each other, I went on ahead, determined to forge my own merry way down the slopes. The mantra I chanted in my mind was *I've got this.*

Before you get the idea that I was a well-trained skier who was familiar with this course because my family visited every year, let me assure you that I was not and we had not. A few days of ski school comprised my training, and this was my first time atop this peak. I should also mention I have a terrible sense of direction. My mom feels confident that I could get lost in a closet if you spun me around a few times.

So there I was on top of the mountain, and instead of waiting for my mom and sister, I set off on my own.

Immediately, I took a wrong turn. The speed bumps in the snow alerted me to my wrong turn. I was looking for the slopes that were flat and easy. This one was not.

No reason to panic, I thought. *I'll figure something out.* As I surveyed my surroundings, I noticed something that reminded me of a climbing wall. You know the ones. They have places to put your feet and things to grab hold of as you climb up. Sure, this wall was made of ice, and no, it didn't have places built in to grab hold of, but it wasn't that tall, and my only other option was the slope with speed bumps. So up the ice I climbed.

I tossed my skis and poles up to the slope I had intended to be on in the first place; then I plowed my snow boots into the ice and started to ascend.

Once atop the wall, I needed to catch up to my mom and sister.

The slope I now found myself on was flat, and that was a wonderful thing. I drew on what I had learned during my few hours of ski school and assumed a pose I believed would make me aerodynamic. I bent my knees and tucked my elbows to my sides. As I skied along the flatter terrain, the wind cascaded over my head and down my back. I felt sure I'd catch up any minute now.

About that time, I rounded a small curve on the flat slope. Out of the corner of my eye, I spotted my mom and sister. They had stopped, maybe to wait on me. I was, remember, skiing at an aerodynamic pace, so I saw them … as I flew right past them.

I didn't encounter a steep hill, but it was a hill I wasn't prepared for and was skiing too fast to handle, so I tumbled, head over heels down the hill. You know those cartoons where the animated coyote turns into a giant snowball and all you can see are his arms and legs poking out the sides? I can assure you that you don't actually turn into a snowball. Not even a little bit.

A nice stranger (who was going the proper speed down the hill) collected my skis and poles and delivered them to me. You might think that by now I'd learned my lesson, but you'd be wrong. I suppose I thought things couldn't get any worse. I gathered myself, my skis, and my poles, stood up on my wobbly legs, and just kept going … right up until the moment I took yet another wrong turn … onto another slope with speed bumps.

This time, I found no way out. There was no ice wall to climb, no easy slope to get back on, no way to keep going. I lay down flat on my back and waited for someone to help me. It was from this position that I determined I did not, in fact, "have this" after all.

It may seem hard to comprehend why I was so stubborn on the mountain that day. I mean, *come on*, how hard is it to slow down, go the right way, and wait on your family? You may have even been shaking your head as you read about my continuous wrong turns down the slope. Too often, though, I'm afraid we approach the details of daily life in a way not all that different from my disaster on the mountain.

We set off on our own and rely on ourselves to get by. When things go wrong, we try to figure it out. When we fall behind, we find ways to catch up. When life falls apart, we put our heads down and just keep going. All the while living broken, separate, and incomplete.

I came face to face with this reality several years ago when my Christmas tree fell over. The whole tree—ornaments, lights, star on top—fell to the ground like a tree on the forest floor. It started when the kids were "playing" with our cat. I don't guess the cat wanted to play, so he took refuge in the Christmas tree. The kids followed the cat into the tree, of course, and the tree came tumbling down. It made quite a mess, but it also identified something in my heart that was much more than a mess.

The truth was, that year had been a struggle for me. My family and I had moved for the sixth time in a span of only ten years, and my days were spent primarily in my home with our young children. I would share a smile or exchange a kind word with a neighbor from time to time, but with family far away, a husband who worked long hours, and no real community to speak of, I felt especially tired and lonely. I spent each new day figuring out how to handle obstacles, catching up in the places where I'd fallen behind, and pushing forward even when things felt like they were falling apart. On this day, though, I was out of options.

Every year for a decade, we had gone as a family to pick out a Christmas tree. We brought it home and hung our ornaments, finishing it off with the same star on top. To me, the tree represented something stable, certain, and whole. So that year as we hung ornaments on the Christmas tree, it felt a little more like I was hanging my heart on the tree. When I found the tree in a shattered pile on the floor, it felt like everything stable and certain in my life was also in a shattered pile on the floor. Beautiful ornaments were crushed. Bright lights had dimmed. A star that once topped the tree now lay separated and alone on the floor.

I felt just like that star.

Maybe you know what I'm talking about. A recent study reported that nearly half of Americans said they felt lonely or left out "sometimes or always,"[1] and the church is not insulated from this problem. One recent study reported that one in three practicing Christians stopped attending church during the COVID-19 pandemic. This study defines "practicing Christians" as people who believe "faith is very important in their lives" and had attended church prior to the pandemic. This same study reports that those no longer attending church "bear more emotional burdens."[2]

Mental, emotional, and even physical health benefits abound for those living in strong community with one another.[3] When we belong to Jesus, we also enjoy the powerful spiritual benefits that come from living in community with other believers.

Because we belong to Jesus, we do not have to live anxious, alienated, and alone. Instead, we can live in community and on mission for Him. When we belong to Jesus, we belong to His body.

However, apart from the body of Christ (which is another name for the church), our lives can feel like a puzzle with a missing piece. You know the feeling. You take the puzzle pieces out of the box and keep the picture on the box lid in view. One by one, you begin to match the pieces together, and you can start to see the finished product as it forms. Anticipation builds as you await that fulfilling moment of putting the final piece in place.

And then it happens: With only one spot left to complete the whole picture, you run out of pieces. There are no more to be found, though you turn the room upside down looking for it. No matter how amazing the rest of the puzzle looks, you can't enjoy what's there because all you can see is what's missing.

As you work through each day of this study, you'll learn that to most deeply experience belonging in the body of Christ, you need to:

- shift your identity from your scars to your Savior,
- put down your own independent ways so you can pull together with others for the cause of Christ,
- press into the body of Christ instead of pulling away from it—especially when life falls apart—and
- cultivate conditions that grow you from "fine" to flourishing.

Right now, you may be thinking about all the frustrations you've had with people lately. You may be cataloging the wrongs that have been done to you, the harmful words that have been said, or the lack of care that has been shown. You may even be thinking you're doing fine on your own and that any belonging to be found in the body of Christ might not be worth the work.

Here's what I've discovered: our quest to keep it together will eventually cause us to fall apart. What you'll learn over the course of the next five weeks is that there is a peace, security, and purpose that is most completely realized when you engage with other believers in the body of Christ.

Here are a few things to help you as you work through this Bible study:

- The first video session is an introduction. After watching it, you'll begin your first week of personal study. To view the videos, follow the link or scan the QR code on the next page.
- Each week is divided into five days of personal study. Days 1–4 include a "Digging In" section designed to take you deeper into the subject we're discussing that day as well as a "Work It Out" section to help you apply what you're learning.
- Day 5 is different from the other days. It discusses something specific we can do together as we pursue belonging in the body of Christ. Day 5 is a little shorter, and you will be prompted to spend time journaling.
- Each week concludes with a video session. You can watch these sessions individually or with a group.

I did make it down the mountain that day, but not on my own. After a little while of lying all alone, my sister skied by and recognized me. She yelled my name, and I called back to confirm: Yes, it was me, and yes, I needed help. Together, we found a way to connect our poles and form a makeshift ladder. She held one end while I climbed up from the other end, and in spite of how ridiculous it must have looked, I made it back up to the place I'd wanted to be all along.

We went the rest of the way together. It wasn't always easy, and I'm pretty sure we slid part of the way down on our bottoms, but we did make it down the mountain … together.

There is a peace, security, and purpose that is most completely realized when you engage with other believers in the body of Christ.

Through many years of trying to handle life all on my own, I've come to realize that I don't want a life that's handled—I want a life that's whole. In spite of our brokenness, we can find our place in the body of Christ.

I want to share with you what God has taught me. As we begin this study, imagine that you and I are up on that mountain. This study is me extending my pole. Grab hold and climb up. We'll go the rest of the way together.

VIDEO SERIES ACCESS
Link: DavidCCook.org/access
Access code: SheBelongs

Scan this code with your mobile
device in camera mode.

Introduction Group Time

Use this suggested schedule and these questions for your first group session.

Welcome

- Ask each member to introduce herself.

Icebreaker Questions

- What drew you to this study?
- Have you ever felt like you're trying to do life all on your own?
- How has feeling isolated or alone impacted your life or your walk with Jesus?

Watch the Introduction video.

Discussion Questions

- In the introduction, Katy said, "Our quest to keep it together will eventually cause us to fall apart." How have you seen this happen in your life?
- In what ways has it affected your present circumstances?
- Read Ephesians 4:1–16. What are some words that stood out to you in this passage of Scripture?
- Do you see any of the things we just read in your life right now? What would you like to have that you feel you don't?
- How are you feeling as we begin this study? Expectant and excited? Cautious and guarded?

Close in Prayer

- Ask for prayer requests, and thank God for this time together.
- Ask God to help you find freedom in His Word and a place in His church.

Reminders for Each Upcoming Week

- Each week, read through days 1–5.
- Confirm your next meeting date and time.

Week 1

The First Step to Belonging

Memory Verse

*He himself bore our sins in his body on the tree,
that we might die to sin and live to righteousness.
By his wounds you have been healed.*

1 Peter 2:24

Introduction

He burst through the door with her in his arms. The look on his face alerted me that something was very wrong.

Moments before, my daughter had been playing in the driveway. She'd been riding her bike alongside her older brothers on a beautiful spring day. All was well until our daughter followed her big brothers down a hill that proved to be too steep for our youngest bike rider. She hit a bump and lost control, sending her face-first over the handlebars. Her jaw hit the pavement, and her cry followed the impact—a cry that initiated her daddy's response.

My husband, Luke, rushed to our little girl's side and without hesitation scooped her up in his arms. He had only one focus: to help our daughter. He carried her into the house and started tending to her wounds. She was bleeding and bruised, crying and afraid. With a damp cloth in hand, Luke knelt next to her and gently wiped the blood away. Once we could see the wounds clearly, we put ointment on them and bandaged them, but we knew her injuries would require professional attention.

The next several hours included a visit to the emergency room and the consultation of specialists. No matter where we were—a waiting room, a doctor's office, or the couch in our own living room—Luke stayed at our daughter's side. He held her if he could, but when she needed to sit on a hospital bed for evaluation and care, he pulled his chair as close to her as possible so she could rest her head on his shoulder.

X-rays and CT scans revealed she had broken her jaw in three places. We were scheduled for a procedure that involved wiring her jaw shut so it could heal, but because her accident had happened over the weekend, we would have to wait until the next morning for the procedure.

As we attempted to sleep that night, my husband and I made a bed of blankets and pillows in our room so our daughter could be near us as she slept. One small whimper from our sleeping girl, though, moved her daddy out of the bed so he could once again scoop her up in his arms.

He held her the rest of the night.

I don't know how much Luke slept, but despite the trauma of the day, our daughter slept peacefully through the night in her father's arms.

The following morning, we went for the procedure. To reduce the risk of further injury, the doctor placed wires in our daughter's mouth to rest her teeth together and provide stability for her bones. On the car ride home, with several weeks ahead of a new diet and a new normal, Luke couldn't bear to let our daughter sit in the back seat alone. And so, as was his habit, he climbed into the back seat so he could scoop her up again and hold her in his arms.

Day 1

A Place for Your Broken Pieces

Memory Verse

*He himself bore our sins in his body on the tree, that we might die to sin
and live to righteousness. By his wounds you have been healed.*
1 Peter 2:24

During the hours and days that followed my daughter's bicycle accident, she found security and rest in the arms of her daddy. In spite of her broken jaw and everything that came with it, in her father's arms she found peace. She was where she belonged.

In the space below, describe what a life of belonging looks like to you.

One definition of belonging is "the feeling of security and support when there is a sense of acceptance, inclusion, and identity for a member of a certain group."[1] Based on this definition, shade in the bar below to show how close or how far away you feel from belonging in the body of Christ.

I don't feel like I belong at all.	I don't feel completely distant, but I don't feel included either.	I feel completely secure and supported in the body of Christ.

What, if anything, keeps you from believing you could live a life of belonging with Jesus and His body?

You may have experienced a broken relationship with a spouse, a friend, a child, or a fellow member of the body of Christ. Past sins may have shattered your hopes of ever being acceptable to God. Maybe it's not your own brokenness you're grappling with but the brokenness of a world that's unraveling all around you. You may have read headlines about church conflict or pondered social media disputes that come across your feed and concluded it's not really possible to belong anywhere this side of heaven.

It's true: There is a security that will be found only when sin is no more and we dwell eternally in the perfect presence of God. However, I believe we can exist in a broken world and still experience belonging. Belonging isn't the absence of brokenness—it's the presence of a Healer.

My goal for this study is for us to live what Paul described in Ephesians 4:16:

> He makes the whole body fit together perfectly. As each part does its own special work, it helps the other parts grow, so that the whole body is healthy and growing and full of love. (NLT)

What words jump out to you in this verse?

Words like *whole, fit together, special work, healthy, growing,* and *full of love* seem so rich with promise, but they may sound quite the opposite of how you feel right now. That's okay. You're right where you need to be because belonging begins in the midst of our brokenness. The first step to belonging is to let God into the broken places of your heart.

My daughter's response to her father's care probably doesn't surprise you. We recognize the blessing of a loving father who ran to his child and comforted her. We would expect her to receive that gift gladly and rest in it. But when circumstances shatter our lives, instead of allowing God to scoop us up, care for us, and put our broken pieces back together, we sometimes pull away.

With six children in my house, there are lots of scrapes and cuts to tend to. Sometimes, one of our children skins his knee or scrapes his elbow. Instead of allowing us to care for the wound, he covers it and recoils. It hurts, and he's afraid that our care will only hurt more. He doesn't want anyone to touch his wound or get near it, so he pulls away and tries to hide it. That feels like the safest option for his pain.

Maybe you feel more like my boy who pulls away. You're not yet convinced that being in Christian community is worth it, and you're worried that if you peel back the bandage covering your past hurts, failures, weaknesses, and sin, you might just fall apart and no one will be there to help you put the pieces back together. If that's you, I understand the resistance you feel right now. But before you decide this isn't for you, let me share something God has taught me.

For a long time I instinctively tried to hide any pain or brokenness in my life, but God began to pull back the makeshift bandages I had placed over my wounds. I didn't understand why we had to do this. It felt so much safer to keep them covered up. But God gently revealed to me the infections that penetrate untreated heart wounds. As with an untreated physical wound, untreated heart wounds grow more and more tender. Though covered up, the wounds get worse, and if they're not treated, infection will spread and create even more hurt.

God doesn't want you to spend your life endlessly trying to keep it together. He wants to heal you, fill you, and lead you to the rest found in His arms when you belong to Him.

Read the verses below, and underline what they say about God's response to our brokenness.

Psalm 34:18 ⟶ "The LORD is near to the brokenhearted and saves the crushed in spirit."

Psalm 147:3 ⟶ "He heals the brokenhearted and binds up their wounds."

How does the truth in these verses change your perspective on brokenness?

What comfort it is to read that God is near to us when we are brokenhearted! He saves us, heals our pains, and comforts our sorrows. I love how *The Message* paraphrases Psalm 34:18: "If your heart is broken, you'll find GOD right there; if you're kicked in the gut, he'll help you catch your breath."

Because God is faithful to comfort and able to heal, you don't have to hide or ignore the broken places of your heart. Instead, you can release your shattered heart to Him and receive the nearness and healing of the Lord.

DIGGING IN

Read Psalm 34:8–10:

> Oh, taste and see that the LORD is good!
>   Blessed is the man who takes refuge in him!
> Oh, fear the LORD, you his saints,
>   for those who fear him have no lack!
> The young lions suffer want and hunger;
>   but those who seek the LORD lack no good thing.

What does the first line of these verses tell us to do?

The Hebrew word translated "taste" is often used to express the tasting of food, but in this verse it's a slightly different concept. Here, it's used to communicate the idea of perceiving something.[2] When David wrote, "Taste and see that the LORD is good," he was writing about something you discover by experience. I love how the Good News Translation presents this idea: "Find out for yourself how good the LORD is" (Ps. 34:8).

Think of something you've found out for yourself. Maybe it was a problem you figured out how to solve on your own or directions to a new place you discovered for yourself. Maybe you researched and learned a new skill on your own, or maybe you refused to take someone else's word about a roller-coaster ride, so you rode it to find out for yourself how exciting it was.

What did you do? Why did you do it? How did you feel once you had experienced it? Use the space below to describe that experience.

If you're like me, you'd much rather find things out for yourself than take someone else's word for it. It's not all that different from what I did that dreadful day on the ski slope. (If you don't know what I'm talking about, go back and read the introduction to this study.)

Think for a moment, though, about how the experience you just described compares with your experience of God. Have you found out for yourself how good the Lord is, or are you taking someone else's word for it?

Read Psalm 34:18 again: "The LORD is near to the brokenhearted and saves the crushed in spirit." Some translators feel that the phrase "crushed in spirit" is connected to the humility that comes from repentance and a contrite heart.[3]

Belonging isn't the absence of brokenness; it's the presence of a Healer.

This is similar to what we read about in Psalm 51:17, where David wrote, "The sacrifices of God are a broken spirit; a broken and contrite heart, O God, you will not despise." The words of Psalm 51 came from the anguish of a heart that had sinned against God. David wrote these words in response to being confronted by the prophet Nathan about David's adultery with Bathsheba and the murder of her husband.

Whether we're choosing to hope in God in the midst of broken circumstances or appealing to God in the brokenness of our sin, our response remains the same: *Taste and see that the Lord is good!* To better understand this, let's go back to my daughter's story and what happened as her broken jaw healed.

After her jaw had been wired shut, my little girl required a liquid diet. The task of finding *one* meal for my daughter to drink was so difficult—and she was going to need three weeks of such meals. Needless to say, this challenge left me concerned.

The first meal I served her through a straw we named "the pizza drink." It was really just tomato soup blended well, but anytime you can add "pizza" to a title, it sounds so much tastier. After a few days, we landed on a favorite breakfast drink too. Because it was her favorite color, we named it "the pink drink," and it immediately became a staple. She liked most sweet, fruit-filled drinks, but after a few days of mostly fruit smoothies, her new diet began to take its toll on her body.

She felt dizzy and emotional, and her already lean body grew even thinner. We tried heartier drinks like chicken soup and chocolate-peanut butter shakes, but she didn't want them. We practically begged her to drink them, but she wouldn't. Maybe she didn't like the color. Maybe she didn't like the smell. Maybe she thought it was too thick or too thin. I don't really know, but somehow she came to the conclusion that the new drinks weren't good, and no matter how bad my six-year-old felt or how much she needed the nutrition, she wouldn't drink them.

After several days of failed attempts to convince my little girl to sip something new, we finally found an answer. One night, she decided she loved blended up chicken pot pie. She took one sip and was hooked. *Hallelujah!* I have no explanation other than we had prayed desperately for God to help us nourish her. She drank a lot of chicken pot pie over the next few weeks, and the more she drank, the less she complained of feeling dizzy or tired. She tasted and saw that what we offered her was good.

To taste God's goodness and experience the belonging that can be found only in Him, we must first be willing to try it. Tasting is something no one else can do for you. Sure, I can take a bite and tell you just how wonderful it is, but only you can taste it for yourself.

So let me do just that: Friend, I've tasted and seen that the Lord is good. He's better than anything I've ever tried. And He's left me so full, I don't need to try anything else. If I could sit across the table from you right now, I'd slide God's Word your way and say, "You have to try this!"

The first step to belonging is to bring your brokenness to Jesus. Instead of tirelessly trying to fix things yourself, taste and see that He is good. Let Him heal you and bind your wounds. Let Jesus put the broken pieces of your heart back together.

WORK IT OUT

Each day will end with a section called "Work It Out." This section is designed to help you process and apply what we've talked about that day. As we begin our study together, read this excerpt from the book *Streams in the Desert*:

> GOD uses most for His glory those people and things which are most perfectly broken. The sacrifices He accepts are broken and contrite hearts....
>
> It was when Jesus took the five loaves and broke them, that the bread was multiplied in the very act of breaking, sufficient to feed five thousand. It was when Mary broke her beautiful alabaster box, rendering it

henceforth useless, that the pent-up perfume filled the house. It was when Jesus allowed His precious body to be broken to pieces by thorns and nails and spear, that His inner life was poured out, like a crystal ocean, for thirsty sinners to drink and live....

And thus, on and on, through all history, and all biography, and all vegetation, and all spiritual life, God must have BROKEN THINGS.

Those who are broken in wealth, and broken in self-will, and broken in their ambitions, and broken in their beautiful ideals, and broken in worldly reputation, and broken in their affections, and broken ofttimes in health; those who are despised and seem utterly forlorn and helpless, the Holy Ghost is seizing upon, and using for God's glory.[4]

Use the space below to write a prayer surrendering any places you've been trying so hard to keep together. Tell God your frustrations or fears, and ask Him to help you trust Him in your brokenness and heal you.

Day 2

When You Don't Feel Accepted

Memory Verse

He himself bore our sins in his body on the tree, that we might die to sin and live to righteousness. By his _____ you have been _____.

1 Peter 2:24

I passed her as I exited the room. She retracted a little as I walked by, then darted into the room I had just left.

Armed with a can of disinfectant, she sprayed the room I had occupied minutes before. Long before the days when we knew of a term called COVID-19, I had come to work sick, and there was no hiding it. My face told the story. Sunken eyes, a pale complexion, and probably a red-tinted nose … and if that weren't enough, I carried a box of tissues with me everywhere I went. No one wanted to approach me. Whether they had their own health in mind or something else, my sniffles and cough were enough to send my coworkers running in the opposite direction.

I worked long hours at a television station. Fresh out of college, with no family or other responsibilities, my focus was on my work, and my dad had taught me to work hard.

So, on the day I woke up not feeling well, I remembered a day when my dad hadn't felt well. As I recall, he sat in his office at the television station he worked at throughout my childhood. He shivered with chills caused by a high fever and burrowed underneath a blanket. All the while, he worked to prepare for the evening news. Only a few hours later, he sat behind a desk on live television with a smile that never even hinted at his sick state. And so, with this in mind, I went to work.

It never crossed my mind no one would want me there.

Ephesians 4:16 details something very different than my state that day: "He makes the whole body fit together perfectly. As each part does its own special work, it helps the other parts grow, so that the whole body is healthy and growing and full of love" (NLT).

This paints the picture of a vibrant, healthy, thriving group of people, full of life and full of love. Sometimes, though, I think we feel more like I did that day at the office. Our circumstances are better described as "barely getting by," and the people around us seem to keep their distance.

We hide our brokenness, and we distance ourselves from others, all the while consoling ourselves that this is how others want it too. We're convinced that no one wants to be around us in our brokenness, so we separate ourselves at all costs until we're fixed. The problem is, we can't fix ourselves.

But the good news is, we don't have to.

When it feels like everyone runs away from your brokenness, Jesus moves toward you. Jesus doesn't grab a can of disinfectant spray and keep His distance—He *is* the disinfectant spray. Read the passages below, and record the kind of brokenness Jesus moved toward.

Mark 5:1–13 ⟶

Mark 5:35–43 ⟶

Beyond demon possession and death, the Gospels record countless healings. Look up the verses below, and connect them to other kinds of brokenness Jesus embraced.

Mark 6:53–56	leprosy
Mark 1:40–42	sickness
Matthew 15:29–31	lame, blind, crippled, mute

Now that we've seen these examples of how Jesus embraced brokenness and uncleanness, let's look deeper at an exchange between a woman and Jesus and how He met her in her brokenness.

DIGGING IN

Read Mark 5:25–26: "There was a woman who had had a discharge of blood for twelve years, and who had suffered much under many physicians, and had spent all that she had, and was no better but rather grew worse."

What was the woman suffering from?

What had she done because of her condition?

What was the result of her seeking help?

The Bible doesn't describe this woman as broken, but I think we can agree that's how she might've felt. For twelve years she had bled. She had sought help. She had spent all that she had. And yet, she had only gotten worse. I imagine she must have felt exhausted, discouraged, and hopeless.

Read verses 27–28: "She had heard the reports about Jesus and came up behind him in the crowd and touched his garment. For she said, 'If I touch even his garments, I will be made well.'"

In the midst of her sickness and hopelessness, what did the woman do?

Why did she do it?

The woman's brokenness compelled her to come to Jesus. But it wasn't just her brokenness that brought her there—it was also her faith.

The New Testament speaks about people touching the edge, or hem, of Jesus' garment and experiencing healing immediately. In Matthew's recording of one such event, he included this detail about the edge, or fringe, of the garment: "A woman who had suffered from a discharge of blood for twelve years came up behind him and touched the fringe of his garment" (Matt. 9:20).

At the close of the Old Testament, Malachi wrote, "For you who fear my name, the sun of righteousness shall rise with healing in its wings. You shall go out leaping like calves from the stall" (4:2). The Hebrew word translated "wings" in Malachi could also be translated "borders" or "corner"—similar to the fringe of a garment.[1] When the woman who reached out to Jesus' hem exclaimed, "If I touch even his garments, I will be made well" (Mark 5:28), she issued a statement of faith that Jesus was the promised Messiah, the Savior sent from God whom they had been waiting for. Let's see what happened next.

Read verses 29–30: "Immediately the flow of blood dried up, and she felt in her body that she was healed of her disease. And Jesus, perceiving in himself that power had gone out from him, immediately turned about in the crowd and said, 'Who touched my garments?'"

Because Jesus had come into contact with the woman's uncleanness, it could've meant that He Himself had become unclean. And for a rabbi to become unclean in the society in which Jesus lived would have been disastrous.[2] Yet Jesus drew attention to the fact that He had touched uncleanness. Jesus didn't shy away from uncleanness. But it gets even better!

Read verse 34: "He said to her, 'Daughter, your faith has made you well; go in peace, and be healed of your disease.'"

There is so much packed into this one sentence, but I want to draw your attention to three words:

daughter ... peace ... healed

When Jesus called this woman "daughter," He identified her. Up to this point, she had been a woman known only by her brokenness. But with one word, Jesus changed all of that. Now she was His, a daughter of the King.

The next word, *peace*, is something we will spend a lot more time discussing in week 3 of our study. But for now, I want you to know two things:

1. There is a wholeness associated with this kind of peace that we can find only in Jesus.
2. Jesus told her to *go* in peace. By this word, He sent her back to the people who had known her only in her sickness but now would see her walking in this new identity and peace.

Third, let's look at the word *healed*. If we also look at the phrase "go in peace," we see that her healing was a catalyst that sent her as a witness to others. When Jesus healed someone's brokenness, it often led them to others.

I think now is a good time to discuss the difference between God's healing hand and Satan's poking finger. Satan wants us to keep our brokenness hidden. He wants to remind us at every turn of how bad it hurts. He wants us to believe it would be dangerous—even disastrous—to let Jesus in and to connect with others who share our identity. So he pokes at the wounds beneath our ineffective bandages, hoping we'll keep them hidden and bound up so they can continue to fester and become more and more infected.

Jesus' healing hand is very different. Our brokenness doesn't keep us from Him. Our feelings of rejection aren't enough to separate us from Him or His body. While it may feel easier, safer, or more natural to guard the broken pieces of our lives, today I invite you to bring your broken pieces to Jesus and His body.

WORK IT OUT

As we seek the belonging found in Jesus and the body of Christ, you are, I hope, becoming more and more willing to be broken. Our goal, though, is not simply to *deal* with the brokenness. When we experience brokenness, we can choose to deal with it our way or bring it to Jesus and let Him be our healer.

To help you identify whether you're simply dealing with your brokenness or bringing your broken pieces to God to let Him heal you, consider these indicators of each:

Feel ⟶ deal
- You think things inwardly but refuse to say or show them outwardly.
- Your thoughts center around me and I.
- You focus on hiding, guarding, or defending the places you feel broken.
- When you feel pain, you don't allow your feelings to advance; instead, you dismiss or downplay them.

Feel ⟶ heal
- You're honest about how you feel because you trust Jesus can heal you.
- Your thoughts center around thanking Jesus for His sacrifice and worshipping Him.
- You focus on spending more time in God's Word and seeking to see others the way He sees them.

Day 3

Fixing It All

Memory Verse

He himself bore our _____ in his _____ on the tree, that we might die to sin and live to righteousness. By his _____ you have been _____.

1 Peter 2:24

After circling this issue for months, we were out of time. We called a family meeting to settle the matter, once and for all.

One by one, the kids raised their hands to establish where they stood. Gathered around the table, we posed the question weighing on all our minds: *What should we name this baby boy?*

Though we were already deep into my pregnancy with our fifth child, we were still struggling to find a name. Luke and I narrowed the options down to three names, but we still needed help picking *the* name. That's when we called on the voices of the older siblings. After everyone had had their say, we ended up with a unanimous vote for the name Isaiah. (Well, almost unanimous. One brother voted for "Jesus" on a write-in ballot, but we decided to go with the majority.)

I love remembering the stories of how we named each of our kids. I love *saying* their names. It's so much more than a word to me. It's a declaration of who they are and how much I love them. It's a connection between their hearts and mine. At its most basic level, however, it identifies them. In school, on the inside of a jacket or on the back of a sports jersey, their name identifies who they are, who they belong to, and what belongs to them.

In the jar below, write on the ice cubes the words you would use to identify yourself. (You can write more than one word on each cube.)

Oftentimes, we identify ourselves according to our stage of life or place of work. You may have put words in the jar like *nurse*, *mother*, or *college student*. When we fill out a form, we're often asked to identify ourselves based on things like age, race, gender, and marital status.

Sometimes, our brokenness can even become a part of our identity. We can identify ourselves based on past or present experiences and the scars they left behind. These identifiers don't always present themselves as easily as the others, so I want you to pause for a moment and ask God to help you see things you may not notice on your own. Go back to the jar, and add any more words God reveals.

When we wrap our identity in our scars, we live broken lives, robbed of the blessings of belonging in the body of Christ. The belonging that comes from letting God into the broken places in our lives requires us to shift our identity from our scars to our Savior.

DIGGING IN

Read Ephesians 4:1, and underline the words Paul uses to identify himself: "I therefore, a prisoner for the Lord, urge you to walk in a manner worthy of the calling to which you have been called."

In this verse, Paul identifies himself based on a circumstance he is currently experiencing. Paul wrote this letter from prison, where he had been confined because he'd been preaching the gospel of Jesus. Let's go back to the opening words of the letter to discover some other words he used to identify himself.

Read Ephesians 1:1–2: "Paul, an apostle of Christ Jesus by the will of God, To the saints who are in Ephesus, and are faithful in Christ Jesus: Grace to you and peace from God our Father and the Lord Jesus Christ."

In these verses, Paul identifies both himself and the people to whom he is writing. How does Paul identify himself in these verses?

How does he identify the Ephesians?

Paul identified himself as an apostle *of* Christ and identified the Ephesians as faithful *in* Christ. The two words *in Christ* describe a state of identity that happens when we follow Jesus and make Him Lord and Savior of our lives.

Fill in the chart below with what the listed verses say about who you were before you were united with Christ and who you are because you are in Christ.

	WHO YOU WERE	WHO YOU ARE
Ephesians 2:1–7		
Ephesians 2:11–16		
Ephesians 4:17–24		

According to the verses you just read, we all have one thing in common: we share a common brokenness. We all have a column titled "Who You Were before Christ." However, the verses above also reveal that when we belong to Jesus, we don't stay in our common brokenness. In Christ, we receive a new common identity.

Paul spent the first three chapters of Ephesians discussing the transformation that happens when we come to salvation in Christ. The first verse of Ephesians 4 marks a shift in the letter. Here, Paul wants followers of Jesus to do something about their new identity. Let's read it again: "I therefore, a prisoner for the Lord, urge you to walk in a manner worthy of the calling to which you have been called." Underline the words that describe what Paul urges his audience to do.

New identity produces changed activity. To respond to the calling to which He has called us, we need to put on our new identity.

In the earlier graphic, the ice cubes fill a portion of the jar. But even if you stacked ice cubes that identify you to the top of the jar, it would not be full. There would still be gaps between cubes. Identity in Christ is like water poured over those ice cubes, filling the whole jar. (To be fair, where I'm from, we would probably pour sweet tea over the ice cubes.)

I love how Paul David Tripp explains the life-changing shift that happens when Jesus becomes our identity. In his book *New Morning Mercies*, Tripp wrote,

> Jesus didn't simply come to rescue disembodied souls. Yes, he saves our souls from eternal damnation, and for that we should be eternally grateful. But he also came to unleash his powerful restoring grace as far as the furthest effect of sin. He came to restore every single thing that sin has broken. He came to fix it all![1]

Jesus came to fix it all. Go back to the first day of this week's study, and recall how you answered the question "What keeps you from believing you could live a life of belonging with Jesus and His body?" How does the fact that Jesus came to fix it all help you see these things differently?

As we close today's study about our identity in Christ, let's read a few verses from a letter Paul wrote to the church in Corinth. Read 1 Corinthians 11:23–24:

> I received from the Lord that which I also delivered to you: that the Lord Jesus on the same night in which He was betrayed took bread; and when He had given thanks, He broke it and said, "Take, eat; this is My body which is broken for you; do this in remembrance of Me." (NKJV)

What did Jesus do with the bread?

What did Jesus say the bread represented?

On what night did Jesus say and do these things?

As they partook in what we now call the Last Supper, on the very night when one of the men who walked closest with Jesus during His time on earth would betray Him, Jesus broke bread and told His disciples, "Take, eat; this is My body which is broken for you."

Jesus knew what it meant to be broken. Because of His scars, we don't have to be defined by ours. Because of Jesus' broken body, we can belong in the body of Christ. I'm excited to talk more with you about that tomorrow.

> *The belonging that comes from letting God into the broken places in our lives requires us to shift our identity from our scars to our Savior.*

WORK IT OUT

Today, we talked about being a jar filled to the brim with identity in Christ. But you may feel more like a jar tipped over on its side: The identity ice cubes remain in the jar, but the identity of Christ that once filled the jar has spilled out and left you more empty than full.

If that's the case, let me encourage you. During our time around the table as my family voted on the name for the newest member, my daughter raised an important question. She wondered whether she'd still have the same name when she grew up. She worried she might not always be my child and shuddered at the thought that something in life might remove her from the place of the daughter I named and so deeply love. I reassured her no matter where she goes or how big she grows, her identity as my child would never change.

Whether your jar has run dry or you've never experienced the shift from the brokenness of your sin to belonging in Christ, that can change today. You do not have to remain who you were. Jesus is ready and waiting to pour His defining grace into your heart.

To better grasp your identity in Christ, go to the end of this week's study and look at the resource titled "What It Means to be 'In Christ.'" Read each verse and look for the truth it ties to your new identity in Christ. Then come back here and fill in the chart below.

IN CHRIST, YOU ARE ...	IN CHRIST, YOU HAVE ...

Are any of these things you didn't know or hadn't considered? Pick one or two of these truths, and write each down on a note card or in the notes app on your phone. Read them several times a day, and ask God to show you more and more about what it means to be *in Christ*.

Day 4

Respond to Your Calling

Memory Verse

He himself bore our _____ in his

_____ on the tree, that we might die to

_____ and live to _____. By his

_____ you have been _____.

1 Peter 2:24

My shoelaces were too long, and the hem of my skirt was frayed. You could hardly call it a uniform.

On top of that, the wooden bleachers where I sat with the other girls in the pep squad had never felt more rigid. This was not what I had imagined. It only reminded me of where I really wanted to belong.

I had desperately wanted to be a cheerleader, but I wasn't. Instead, I sat in the stands on the pep squad and watched from a distance as the other girls smiled and cheered and led the crowd. They had real uniforms, something I'm sure had been ordered new out of a catalog. They had hair bows and shoes that matched, and their pom-poms were school colors. From center court they did motions and jumps and pyramids, oh my! Everyone in the stands, including me, watched. We were spectators, not participants.

I also watched from a distance while they talked together, laughed together, and, I'm sure, made plans to hang out together after the pep rally. All of which I had no part in. We went to the same school; we sat in the same classrooms; we even had some of the same friends. But I wasn't a part of what they were doing.

I wanted what they had. I wanted to belong.

Knowing we have identity in Christ is only the beginning of our belonging. To truly experience the fullness found in Jesus, we need to take a vital next step. Because we belong to Jesus, we do not have to live alone, feel aimless, or be anxious. Instead, we can live in community and on mission for Christ.

Paul used a variety of images to refer to the common identity that unites followers of Jesus. Look up the following verses from Ephesians, and match them with some of the ways Paul described the church.

Ephesians 1:22–23   body
Ephesians 2:21   bride
Ephesians 2:19   household
Ephesians 5:31–32   temple

Our identity *in* Christ will always lead us to the body *of* Christ. At the moment we receive salvation through Jesus, we become members of His body. To respond to our calling, we must (1) put on our new identity in Christ and (2) participate in the body of Christ.

It is with this in view that Paul urged the members of the church in Ephesus to "walk in a manner worthy of the calling to which you have been called" (4:1). Paul wrote letters to individuals to instruct them and encourage them (such as Timothy and Titus), but this letter was not written to an individual. This letter was written to a church, a group of people who identified themselves as being *in Christ*. So when Paul exhorts them to "walk in a manner worthy of the calling," it's implied that he means they should do so *together*.

For more about this common identity and the seismic shift that happens because of it, let's read Acts 13:1: "There were in the church at Antioch prophets and teachers, Barnabas, Simeon who was called Niger, Lucius of Cyrene, Manaen a lifelong friend of Herod the tetrarch, and Saul."

What five names are listed in this verse?

Some of the names include descriptors. List those here.

The names listed in this verse include men from different countries, cultures, and backgrounds. This verse gives us some of the words they may have written on their identity cubes.

Barnabas was from Cyprus and Lucius from North Africa. The other name given for Simeon, Niger, is a Roman name that in Latin means "black," which some scholars believe may indicate African origin.

Manaen was possibly the childhood friend of the ruler, Herod, and Saul, known as Paul (and the author of the letter to the Ephesians), was a Jew and trained rabbi.[1] With so many differences, all these people found one thing in common: Jesus.

Their identity in Christ united them.

Read Ephesians 4:15–16:

> Speaking the truth in love, we are to grow up in every way into him who is
> the head, into Christ, from whom the whole body, joined and held together
> by every joint with which it is equipped, when each part is working properly,
> makes the body grow so that it builds itself up in love.

Who is the whole body to grow up into?

How is Jesus described as it relates to the whole body?

Paul pulls the thread of Christ's headship through the entire letter to the Ephesians. He first mentions Christ as the head of the church in chapter 1. Read verses 22–23: "He put all things under his feet and gave him as head over all things to the church, which is his body, the fullness of him who fills all in all."

In these verses, Paul establishes Christ as head over the church, and the words he chooses to describe the church (or the body of Christ) are powerful.

How does Paul describe the church, Christ's body?

The Amplified Bible describes the body of Christ like this: "In that body lives the full measure of Him Who makes everything complete, and Who fills everything everywhere with Himself" (Eph. 1:23b AMPC).

Slow down and really sit with what you just read. In the body of Christ—the body made up of believers in Jesus like you and me—lives the full measure of Jesus, who makes everything complete.

This is describing more than those casual conversations you might have at the coffeehouse when you circle up with people in similar circumstances or life stages. So much more is at stake. Our peace, security, and purpose are most completely experienced and expressed when we respond to our calling together with other believers in the body of Christ.

Because of Jesus, we have a common identity with every other follower of Jesus. That common identity is the starting line for everything we will talk about for the next five weeks. No matter what words you used to identify yourself yesterday, no matter how similar or different they were compared to someone else's words, when we follow Jesus, we all become part of the body of Christ, of which He is the head.

Over the next few weeks, we will spend a lot of time in the book of Ephesians, digging into what it looks like to engage in the body of Christ and the belonging that comes with it. Today, as we begin this journey, let's take a trip back to the Old Testament to find out more about the biblical concept of community—its identity and its purpose.

DIGGING IN

Read Exodus 15:13–18:

> You have led in your steadfast love the people whom you have redeemed;
>> you have guided them by your strength to your holy abode.
> The peoples have heard; they tremble;
>> pangs have seized the inhabitants of Philistia.
> Now are the chiefs of Edom dismayed;
>> trembling seizes the leaders of Moab;
>> all the inhabitants of Canaan have melted away.
> Terror and dread fall upon them;
>> because of the greatness of your arm, they are still as a stone,
> till your people, O LORD, pass by,
>> till the people pass by whom you have purchased.
> You will bring them in and plant them on your own mountain,
>> the place, O LORD, which you have made for your abode,
>> the sanctuary, O Lord, which your hands have established.
> The LORD will reign forever and ever.

How are God's people described at the beginning of the passage above? (Hint: It's the phrase that follows *people*.)

There are more identifying words at the end of verse 16. Record those here:

What does verse 17 say God would do for His covenant people?

The people described in Exodus 15 are the nation of Israel. Israel, a man formerly called Jacob, had twelve sons who became the twelve tribes of Israel. Way back when the group that would one day become the nation of Israel consisted of only one man, Abraham, God promised them a land of their own (see Gen. 12:1–3).

Over the course of their history, the nation of Israel became enslaved in Egypt. In Exodus 15, the people of Israel have just witnessed what God had promised He would do for them through His servant Moses (see 3:10—4:31). Together, Moses and all the children of Israel rejoiced and praised God for parting the Red Sea and freeing them from slavery to the Egyptians.

To grasp this new state of God's people, it's important to understand where they had been. Just a few chapters earlier, Moses told the people of Israel about God's plan to deliver them. But they did not join Moses in praise and celebration. Instead, "They did not listen to Moses, because of their broken spirit and harsh slavery" (6:9b).

The Hebrew word translated "broken spirit" is *qotser*. Depending on what English translation you read, it may be rendered in a variety of ways. Here are some of the other words translators have used to describe this state of brokenness:

- "complete exhaustion" (CEB)
- "impatience and despondency" (AMP)
- "discouragement" (NIV)

One scholar, Robert Wall, elaborated on the significance of God's redemption of Israel from slavery in Egypt: "Israel experienced God's liberating grace as a people, and as a people who were called together to give adequate response to the God who delivered them from slavery and set them on a course to freedom and *šalôm*. Community was first formed, then, to worship God."[2]

God brought His people out of slavery in Egypt to bring them into a community that would both worship Him and be His witness to the surrounding nations. Just as the Israelites were set apart, in Christ we too have been set apart and called into community to worship Jesus and proclaim His praises to the world (see 1 Pet. 2:9).

Before we leave this discussion, I don't want us to miss something that I think is really exciting.

Read Exodus 15:26:

> If you will diligently listen to the voice of the LORD your God, and do that which is right in his eyes, and give ear to his commandments and keep all his statutes, I will put none of the diseases on you that I put on the Egyptians, for I am the LORD, your healer.

Belonging isn't the absence of brokenness; it's the presence of a Healer. The Old Testament community of Israel had a Healer, the sick and bleeding woman we read about on day 2 had a Healer, and you have a Healer too. The good news of Jesus' life, death, and resurrection heals us, restores us, identifies us, and brings us together into one body—the body of Jesus Christ.

WORK IT OUT

In the moments when I've felt the most alienated, God has often led me to take the initiative to walk with someone else. Whether I was watching the cheerleaders while I sat on the bleachers, sitting alone at a preschool Christmas play, or walking into a room where everyone but me seemed to belong, what I've found so many times is that the women around me feel just as alienated as I do. My first step toward walking in our common calling blesses and refreshes both my soul and the soul of my sister who quietly felt like she was walking alone too.

As we try to push past our own feelings of hurt, brokenness, and rejection, here are a few places we can begin:

- **Her acceptance isn't your rejection.** When you see a fellow member of the body of Christ who appears to have vibrant community and belonging in her life, you can choose to be happy for her instead of feeling sorry for yourself.
- **Pray and reach out even if you don't think she's interested.** The woman you see who seems to have all she needs may not have all you think she has. She might not look broken, but that doesn't mean she isn't.
- **Shift your mindset from focusing on what you *don't* have to dwelling on what you *do* have.** With the hurt, brokenness, and pain that can come from relationships, there are also blessings. Somehow, I seem more bent on remembering the bad, and in the meantime I can forget the good that's been given to me.

In the moments when I've felt the most alienated, God has often led me to take the initiative to walk with someone else.

Just as Jesus reached out to us in our brokenness, we can take the first step to reach out to others, even when we still feel alone.

Think of one or two women in your life right now whom you can begin praying for. If you can't think of any, ask God to bring someone to mind. Commit to pray for her each day for the next week, and ask God to show you how you can reach out to her.

Day 5

Do It Together: Walk

Memory Verse

He himself bore our _____in his _____on

the tree, that we might _____to _____

and _____to _____. By his

_____ you have been _____.

1 Peter 2:24

When I answered the door, my face was red and swollen. My tears glistened in the sunlight, and I dared not blink for fear of the waterfall that might cascade from my cheeks and flood my soul. On the other side of the door stood my friend Stephanie with two smoothies. One for me and one for her. Just a few minutes earlier, I had called her with the news, "It's a tumor."

When our second-born son was an infant, we noticed a bump on his skull. It had started as something the doctor called "just soft tissue," but lately it had grown into a noticeable bulge, so we'd arranged to see a pediatric specialist. I don't know what I'd been expecting to hear, but it wasn't those three words, "It's a tumor." We scheduled surgery two weeks out and made arrangements for pre-op visits. But shockwaves rumbled through my soul. *What about right now?* I silently screamed. *What do I do while I wait?*

My fingers quivered as I dialed Stephanie's number. "Do you need me to come over?" she asked. My husband was at work, and our family lived hundreds of miles away, yet I refused her offer. I tried to handle it and just keep going. However, as the reality of going home to an empty house consumed me, I called her back. She took my smoothie order, and minutes after I walked through my door, she knocked.

She sat with me the rest of the afternoon. She didn't pray a prayer that freed me from all my worry and doubt. She didn't bring me a word that assured me everything would be okay. She didn't even fold my laundry or do my dishes. She simply sat with me. She let me unravel and face my deepest fears. She listened to the cry of my heart.

A few weeks later, the surgeon successfully removed the tumor from our son's skull, and the lab found it to be benign. In the following weeks, while our baby wore a bandage that wrapped completely around his head, a carousel of friends tended to us. They brought food, called to check on us, and loved on our little patient. They encouraged us and built us up. They walked with us through the uncertainty of our circumstances.

Many verses in Scripture speak about the need for us to do life together. Here are two examples:

> I no longer call you servants, because a servant does not know his master's business. Instead, I have called you friends, for everything that I learned from my Father I have made known to you. (John 15:15 NIV)

> Only let your manner of life be worthy of the gospel of Christ, so that whether I come and see you or am absent, I may hear of you that you are standing firm in one spirit, with one mind striving side by side for the faith of the gospel. (Phil. 1:27)

To walk in a manner worthy of the calling we have received includes walking together, broken pieces and all.

In the body of Christ, what you'll find is a group of broken people who, healed by Jesus' hand and put together by His life, are made whole. And it may just be that your experience of healing through the love of Jesus is what someone else needs to find the blessing of belonging in the body of Christ.

WORK IT OUT

Day 5 of each week will be different from the other days. Instead of assigning more study, I want to give you this day to reflect upon what you've learned through the week. I'll leave you room to write and process, and I encourage you not to rush through it. I believe this day is as important as the rest.

This is your opportunity to let God reveal broken places in your heart and begin the healing process. You can trust Him with those places. There's nowhere better to begin than in the scarred hands of your Savior.

Use the space below to write down some things about this week that you don't want to forget or things you are still processing through. Is there a step God is asking you to take? Is there a truth about your identity in Christ that you need to put on? What do you need to do to respond to your calling in Christ?

To walk in a manner worthy of the calling we have received includes walking together, broken pieces and all.

What It Means to Be "In Christ"

The first three chapters of Ephesians are aimed at outlining the new identity that believers in Christ receive. Below are several verses from those chapters that mention our identity with the words *in Christ* or *in Him*.

Blessed be the God and Father of our Lord Jesus Christ, who has blessed us in Christ with every spiritual blessing in the heavenly places, even as he chose us in him before the foundation of the world, that we should be holy and blameless before him. (1:3–4)

In him we have redemption through his blood, the forgiveness of our trespasses, according to the riches of his grace. (1:7)

In him we have obtained an inheritance, having been predestined according to the purpose of him who works all things according to the counsel of his will. (1:11)

In him you also, when you heard the word of truth, the gospel of your salvation, and believed in him, were sealed with the promised Holy Spirit. (1:13)

By grace you have been saved—and raised us up with him and seated us with him in the heavenly places in Christ Jesus, so that in the coming ages he might show the immeasurable riches of his grace in kindness toward us in Christ Jesus. (2:5b–7)

We are his workmanship, created in Christ Jesus for good works, which God prepared beforehand, that we should walk in them. (2:10)

Now in Christ Jesus you who once were far off have been brought near by the blood of Christ. (2:13)

In him you also are being built together into a dwelling place for God by the Spirit. (2:22)

This was according to the eternal purpose that he has realized in Christ Jesus our Lord, in whom we have boldness and access with confidence through our faith in him. (3:11–12)

Week 1 Group Time

Welcome

- Leader: Introduce week 1 and ask each member to share anything she underlined or highlighted throughout the week's study.
- Review the memory verse for the week: 1 Peter 2:24.

Watch the week 1 video: "The First Step to Belonging."

Discussion Questions

- Our first step to belonging is to bring our brokenness to Jesus. Read Psalms 34:18 and 147:3. How does the truth in these verses change your perspective on brokenness?
- Describe something you've found out for yourself. Would you say you've found out for yourself that the Lord is good? Why or why not?
- At the end of day 2, Katy discussed the difference between dealing with our brokenness our way and bringing our brokenness to Jesus so He can heal us. What identifiers have you seen in your own life of dealing with or allowing Jesus to heal your brokenness? Do you have any identifiers to add to the list?
- What were some of the words you used to identify yourself on day 3?
- Katy wrote, "Our identity *in* Christ will always lead us to the body *of* Christ." How have you experienced this?
- At the end of day 4, Katy listed three places to begin reaching out to others in the body of Christ. Did you try any of these this week? How did it go?

Close in Prayer

- Ask for prayer requests, and thank God for your time together.
- Ask God to help you respond to your calling in Christ.

Week 2

You Belong Here

Memory Verse

Holy Father, keep them in your name, which you have given me, that they may be one, even as we are one.

John 17:11b

Introduction

They lined up one by one, no questions asked.

They didn't come begrudgingly. They came with an eagerness you could see on their faces. They were ready. They were excited. And they were together.

After several rounds of competition that had stretched throughout the day, the moment had finally arrived. Only two teams remained, and one would soon be crowned champion. The front lawn of our local elementary school was the stage for the epic tug-of-war championship between two fourth grade classes.

The rest of the classes had been beaten. Only these two remained, and while some may call tug-of-war a game, I feel confident the fourth graders holding the rope approached this as anything but a game. This was (tug of) *war*.

Mrs. Johnston's class formed a line down one half of the rope, while the opposing class took their places on the other half. No one argued over who stood by whom, and no one questioned who should be on which side of the rope.

Because I had a daughter in the class, I had heard the stories of disagreements and misunderstandings. I knew all these students weren't best friends. However, whether they never played together at recess or sat next to each other at lunch, in this moment, it didn't matter. There was a tug-of-war championship on the line, and it was one class against another. They needed every hand and body if they wanted to be the strongest they could be.

So whether they were friends or not, one thing remained true: they were all part of Mrs. Johnston's fourth grade class.

Tension built as the PE teacher gripped the middle of the rope. All the students fixed their eyes on his hands. Their bodies leaned back as they waited for the rope to drop. Nearby, teachers held their cameras in position to capture the epic event.

Like a lightning bolt, the teacher dropped the rope, and as though they had practiced for months, the students in Mrs. Johnston's class leaned back as one force. Their shoulders shot backward, and their heels dug into the ground. The other class did the same.

With jaws clenched tight and hands gripped even tighter, every student did their part. They didn't yell at each other or even check to see who wasn't pulling their weight. They each focused on doing as much as they could do to pull their class to victory.

Acting as one, they pushed and pulled and tugged the rope. And in only a matter of seconds, they had successfully moved the middle of the tug-of-war rope across the line that signaled their victory.

Mrs. Johnston's fourth grade class worked as one to win the championship. They celebrated as one too. Classmates jumped, hollered, raised their hands, and showered each other with high fives.

Together, they had done it, and together, they enjoyed it.

Day 1

A Part of the Whole

Memory Verse

Holy Father, keep them in your name, which you have given
me, that they may be one, even as we are one.

John 17:11b

I still smile every time I remember that tug-of-war victory. It was so much fun to watch those kids unite for a common purpose and receive the reward of their hard work together. They set aside their differences with no questions asked because they all knew where they belonged: Mrs. Johnston's fourth grade class.

A few years after that epic face-off, I came across another kind of tug-of-war. As I scoured the internet for Christmas gifts, I stumbled upon something called four-way tug-of-war. I'd never heard of this before, so I investigated.

While this game shared a name with the original, it was very different. Instead of joining with others to pull in the same direction for victory, this version put four people up against one another, and it was every man for himself. Each person pulled in their own direction, and the winner was the one who pulled harder and faster than the others to recover a flag.

In the first kind of tug-of-war, you operate alongside others. You share strength and resources. You encourage each other and strive side by side. If you win, you celebrate together. If you lose, you still come together to encourage each other and evaluate together for the next time.

But in the four-way tug-of-war, you have only yourself to count on—or to fault. You have only *your* strength to draw from and only *your* thoughts to keep you moving. If you win, you celebrate alone. If you lose, you have only yourself to console.

As I considered the disparity between these two tug-of-war games, I couldn't help but think about how these approaches play out in our daily lives. Too often, we pull in our own directions. We face life alone and try to figure it out, catch up, or keep going.

But there is another way. Because we belong to Jesus, we can unite with others to pull together for the cause of Christ.

In the book of Ephesians, Paul repeatedly describes us as members of something. Look up the verses below, and record what Paul says we are members of.

Ephesians 2:19 •———➤

Ephesians 3:6 •———➤

Ephesians 4:25 •———➤

Ephesians 5:30 •———➤

Depending on the source you use, *member* can be defined in a variety of ways. Some of my favorite definitions include "a person … belonging to a particular group"[1] or "a part of a whole."[2]

As followers of Jesus, we no longer live separate and alone, striving for our own way. Instead, we live connected to every other follower of Jesus as fellow members of the body of Christ. We are individually a part of the whole, just as the members of our physical body are dependent upon one another and cannot function separately from each other. Our membership in the body of Christ creates an interdependence on one another that is vital to our belonging.

Read Ephesians 4:4–6:

> There is one body and one Spirit—just as you were called to the one hope
> that belongs to your call—one Lord, one faith, one baptism, one God and
> Father of all, who is over all and through all and in all.

Seven times in these verses, Paul uses the word *one*. In the blanks below, write the words that follow the word *one*.

1. One _____
2. One _____
3. One _____
4. One _____
5. One _____
6. One _____
7. One _____

Belonging brings oneness. In your own words, how do you define oneness?

How do you think oneness is defined as it pertains to the body of Christ?

I recently talked with a woman who grew up in church. She bristled at the thought of oneness. To her, oneness had been communicated in a way that required her to fit into the same mold as everyone else. She believed that to be a follower of Jesus, she had to look the same as every other Christian. She had to drive the same car, wear the same clothes, have the same color hair, and raise the same number of children. Because she wasn't exactly the same as everyone else, she felt discouraged and like she didn't belong. She felt as though she couldn't be one with the body of Christ and still be herself.

This, however, is not the definition of oneness Paul wrote about. It's important that we understand what oneness is and what it is not. Let's dig deeper to find out how the Bible defines oneness.

DIGGING IN

According to Ephesians 4:4–6, oneness in the body of Christ has a source not created by human hands. Today, we looked at seven statements about oneness from Ephesians. A central piece of those statements is the Trinity.[3] Because of this, we can conclude:

> Oneness is a result of the oneness of God.[4]
>
> Oneness is not something we can produce apart from God.

The oneness of God is described as the Trinity. *Trinity* is the word the church has coined to identify God as one being with three distinct parts or persons. The oneness of God is the foundation of our oneness in the body of Christ. The *Tyndale Bible Dictionary* explains the three persons of the Trinity like this:[5]

- God the Father—"The Scriptures present the Father as the source of creation, the giver of life, and God of all the universe (see John 5:26; 1 Cor. 8:6; Eph. 3:14–15)."
- God the Son, Jesus Christ—"The Son is depicted as the image of the invisible God, the exact representation of his being and nature, and the Messiah-Redeemer (see Phil. 2:5–6; Col. 1:14–16; Heb. 1:1–3)."

- God the Spirit or the Holy Spirit—"The Spirit is God in action, God reaching people—influencing them, regenerating them, infilling them, and guiding them (see John 14:26; 15:26; Gal. 4:6; Eph. 2:18)."

Each member of the Trinity is named in the statements about oneness that you wrote down above. Go back to your list, and circle the words *one Spirit, one Lord,* and *one God and Father.* The other statements—*one body, one hope, one faith, one baptism*—describe things that are made possible because of the Trinity.[6]

The oneness of God produces oneness is us. Because we share one Spirit, one Lord, and one God and Father, we need nothing more to be one as a body of Christ. Which leads us to our next truth:

Oneness *does* lead us to the same One.
Oneness *does not* equal sameness.

Jesus demonstrated this idea of oneness when He called His twelve disciples. Read Matthew 10:1–4:

He [Jesus] called to him his twelve disciples and gave them authority over unclean spirits, to cast them out, and to heal every disease and every affliction. The names of the twelve apostles are these: first, Simon, who is called Peter, and Andrew his brother; James the son of Zebedee, and John his brother; Philip and Bartholomew; Thomas and Matthew the tax collector; James the son of Alphaeus, and Thaddaeus; Simon the Zealot, and Judas Iscariot, who betrayed him.

According to verse 1, Jesus called His twelve disciples to _____.

In the following chart, list the names of the twelve disciples Jesus called. Some of the names also include identifiers. Record any identifiers you find in these verses.

DISCIPLE	IDENTIFIER

Jesus' twelve disciples had their differences. Some were fishermen; one was a tax collector, another a revolutionary. Some were brothers; some were strangers. What we know is, they were not the same. They came from different places and had different experiences, but they all came to the same One.

The oneness Paul describes in Ephesians 4 is something we receive when we come into fellowship with God through Jesus. Jesus extends to us the invitation to leave our alienated life of sin, shame, and brokenness and join with the body of Christ. This isn't a demand or a required responsibility of our faith. It's a gift from God.

Because of Jesus, we have been reconciled to God through one faith. Because of Jesus, we have been united into one body. You belong in the body of Christ.

Because we belong to Jesus, we can unite with others to pull together for the cause of Christ.

WORK IT OUT

Go back to the example of the two different tug-of-war games. Which example best describes your approach to life as a Christian right now—the four-way tug-of-war or the original version? Why?

Our willingness to be one with the body of Christ impacts not only *our* lives but also the lives of our brothers and sisters in Christ. When we step up to the rope and pull in the direction of Jesus, other members of Christ's body are helped, strengthened, encouraged, and equipped.

Consider for a moment who may benefit from you picking up the rope and pulling in the same direction with them.

Day 2

Words to Never Forget

Memory Verse

Holy Father, keep them in your name, which you have given me, that they
may be _____, even as we are _____.
John 17:11b

We gathered in a semicircle around his bed in a small, stale room. My sister sat directly across from me, while Mom leaned toward the end of the hospital bed. Though no one had told my dad he had only a few weeks to live, it seemed as if he sensed his time on earth was short. So when he talked, we listened carefully. His words were the only thing that mattered in that moment.

I scooted forward in my chair, assuming a more serious posture, one that communicated not just hearing but really receiving his words. He told my sister and me to take care of our mom after he was gone, and he told us to try not to be sad. As he talked, I nodded. I wanted my dad to know he could count on me to honor his requests. And in the deepest place of my heart, I made a commitment that day to do exactly what my dad asked me to do.

We prayed together and shared memories that brought both tears and laughter. Less than a month later, we again stood near my dad's body, this time to say our final goodbyes. We would never hear his voice again on this side of heaven. All we had to hold on to were the last words he had left us with.

As I write this, it's been more than two years since that day in the hospital room with my dad, yet I still remember it so vividly. I remember what I was wearing. I remember how I entered the room. The details of the day remain so clear, and they still bring up deep emotions—because they were some of the last words I would hear my dad say.

The last words of a loved one are special, aren't they?

The exchange I shared with my dad that day continues to impact my life all this time later. I remember his words, and when I do, it prompts me to consider if I am doing what he asked me to do. I evaluate if I'm living in a way that would make him happy. More than anything, even though he's not here, I still want to make my dad proud. I want to do what he would have wanted me to do.

Our memory verse this week records some of Jesus' last words: "Holy Father, keep them in your name, which you have given me, that they may be one, even as we are one" (John 17:11b).

After this chapter, John's gospel turns to chronicle Jesus' arrest and death on the cross. John 17 truly does record Jesus' last words spoken in a prayer to His Father. Just as I did with my father's last words, I think it's important that we lean into these words of Jesus and consider what was on our Savior's heart in the shadow of the cross. When we do, we find that John 17:11 reveals two important things:

1. In the last hours before His death, Jesus had His disciples on His mind.
2. Jesus' desire for His disciples was that they would be one with each other.

We've learned about our calling to come to God through faith in Jesus. But based on Jesus' words in John 17, we learn there's another part to our calling. You were called to *One*, and you were called to *be one*.

Read Ephesians 4:4–6 again, and underline the three persons of the Trinity:

> There is one body and one Spirit—just as you were called to the one hope that belongs to your call—one Lord, one faith, one baptism, one God and Father of all, who is over all and through all and in all.

Yesterday, we listed the seven "one" statements from these verses and discussed how the Trinity was a central piece. So central, in fact, that Paul bases his entire call for church unity on the idea of one Spirit, one Lord, and one God and Father. Ephesians is packed full of this kind of Trinitarian language.[1] In this letter, Paul emphasizes both the oneness of the Trinity and the oneness necessary for followers of Jesus to walk in a manner worthy of the calling to which we have been called.

Some scholars make an interesting observation as to why they believe Paul is so adamant about the call to oneness in the body of Christ. To understand it, we need to travel back to the road on which Paul encountered Jesus. At the time, Paul's name was Saul, and he was fiercely committed to persecuting followers of Christ. As he traveled to continue his persecution, Jesus intervened, and Saul fell to the ground. Let's read about what happened next:

> Falling to the ground, he heard a voice saying to him, "Saul, Saul, why are you persecuting me?" And he said, "Who are you, Lord?" And he said, "I am Jesus, whom you are persecuting. But rise and enter the city, and you will be told what you are to do." (Acts 9:4–6)

What does Jesus ask Saul?

How does Jesus answer Saul's question, "Who are you"?

Jesus did not say that Saul was persecuting His church. Instead, when Jesus confronted Saul on the road to Damascus, He told Saul, "*You* are persecuting *Me*." It is out of this encounter that scholars believe Paul's concept of, and commitment to, deep unity among believers in the body of Christ was formed.[2]

To learn more about how we are called to be one with each other just as Jesus is one with God, let's scoot up in our chairs, lean in, and listen carefully to more of Jesus' last words.

DIGGING IN

Read John 17:20–23:

> I do not ask for these only, but also for those who will believe in me through their word, that they may all be one, just as you, Father, are in me, and I in you, that they also may be in us, so that the world may believe that you have sent me. The glory that you have given me I have given to them, that they may be one even as we are one, I in them and you in me, that they may become perfectly one, so that the world may know that you sent me and loved them even as you loved me.

On whose behalf does Jesus ask?

What does Jesus say He has given us?

Why does He say He has given us His glory?

Why does Jesus pray for us to become perfectly one? (Hint: The answer follows the words *so that*.)

There's a lot going on in these verses. Jesus is talking about Himself and His relationship to His Father. He's also talking about the way His relationship with His Father impacts His relationship with His followers.

Because there are so many personal pronouns in these three verses, it may be helpful to distinguish between them. If you have highlighters or pens, choose three colors and follow the instructions below. If you don't have highlighters or pens, you can mark the text using different shapes, like a triangle, a circle, and a star.

- Highlight the words *I* and *me* in one color to indicate Jesus is speaking about Himself.
- With a different color or shape, highlight the words *you* and *Father* to show when Jesus is speaking about God.
- Finally, in a third color or shape, highlight the words *they* and *them* to note when Jesus is speaking about His disciples.

In some of His last words, when Jesus prays that His disciples "may all be one, just as you, Father, are in me, and I in you," He calls attention to the oneness of His relationship with His Father.

In his book *The Knowledge of the Holy*, A. W. Tozer says, "The Persons of the Godhead, being one, have one will."[3] He goes on to observe that, "In the Scriptures the three Persons are shown to act in harmonious unity in all the mighty works that are wrought throughout the universe."[4]

Throughout His time on earth, Jesus demonstrated a surrendered will that acted in harmony with the will of His Father. Read the verses below, and underline every reference to Jesus' commitment to His Father's will:

- Jesus said to them, "My food is to do the will of Him who sent Me and to completely finish His work." (John 4:34 AMP)
- Pray then like this: "Our Father in heaven, hallowed be your name. Your kingdom come, your will be done, on earth as it is in heaven." (Matt. 6:9–10)
- I have come down from heaven not to do My own will and purpose but to do the will and purpose of Him Who sent Me. (John 6:38 AMPC)
- He withdrew from them about a stone's throw, and knelt down and prayed, saying, "Father, if you are willing, remove this cup from me. Nevertheless, not my will, but yours, be done." (Luke 22:41–42)

In each of these verses, Jesus surrenders His own will to His Father's. He describes doing His Father's will as His nourishment and purpose, and He submits to His Father's will even when it goes against His own feelings or desires. This is how Jesus was one with His Father, and this is the oneness Jesus spoke of as He prayed that His followers would be one.

Paul wrote this to another early church: "I am sure of this, that he who began a good work in you will bring it to completion at the day of Jesus Christ" (Phil. 1:6). The "you" in the verse refers to the church at Philippi. Compare this verse with: "Jesus said to them, 'My food is to do the will of Him who sent Me and to completely finish His work'" (John 4:34 AMP).

What words or ideas do these verses have in common?

Both of these verses point to a work that will be *completed*. Jesus speaks of the will of His Father and His aim to completely finish that work, and Paul writes about the work God began in the church at Philippi and how He will bring it to completion in them.

The original Greek words for "completion" in these verses are both derived from a word that can be defined as "to carry through completely,… to bring to an end."[5] The oneness Jesus asked for with His last words is much deeper than outward appearances or shared opinions. It involves wholly submitting to God's will, whether we feel like it or not, and allowing Him to work through us to completely finish the work Christ began in His body. To accomplish the oneness Jesus prayed for before He died on the cross for your sins and mine, we must commit to carry out His will *completely*.

As we close today's study, I want to go back to John 17:11 and look at one more thing: "Holy Father, keep *them* in your name, which you have given me, that *they* may be one, even as we are one."

The words *them* and *they* point to Jesus' disciples. Jesus prayed both for His first disciples, the ones present with Him at the time, and for us, those who would believe in Him through their word.

One chapter prior to Jesus' prayer in John 17, Jesus told His disciples they would be scattered and fall away because of His arrest and crucifixion (see John 16:32). Mark's gospel records the sad words confirming that Jesus' prediction came true: "They all left him and fled" (Mark 14:50). Jesus knew that in the wake of His betrayal and arrest, His disciples would scatter. Yet this reality didn't cause Him to lose hope for the belonging He designed for them. Jesus still prayed that they would be one.

The same way I cherished the last words of my earthly father, I don't want to rush past the last words of our Savior. Let's lean into our Savior's words, listen closely, and remember them often. To love Jesus is to love what He loves, and Jesus loves His church. He deeply desires for us to be one … perfectly one.

WORK IT OUT

When we think of Jesus being in us, I think we sometimes envision something smaller existing inside us. When we consider the idea of God being in Jesus and Jesus being in us, perhaps we imagine a stack of boxes that gets progressively smaller. Each time you open a box, you find a smaller box, then a smaller box inside that box, and so on.

The picture Jesus paints in John 17, however, is not that at all. What Jesus describes is a full indwelling. It's not something that exists inside something else but something that consumes every part of something else.

When I imagine Jesus consuming every part of me, it's easier to set aside my own feelings or opinions in order to seek His will and the oneness He desires for His body.

How does shifting your perspective to Jesus consuming every part of you—your thoughts, feelings, and will—help you pursue oneness in the body of Christ?

To love Jesus is to love what He loves, and Jesus loves His church.

Day 3

Something Worth Fighting For

Memory Verse

Holy Father, keep them in your name, which you have given me,
that _____ may be _____, even
as _____ are _____.
John 17:11b

They were important to him, and he didn't want anyone to mess with them.

When one of our boys received a set of building blocks for his birthday, he put them together to create something special. There was just one problem: his younger siblings didn't want to leave his blocks as he had assembled them. Each day, they secretly tried to take the blocks, separate them from the way our son had put them together, and distort them into something entirely different from what he wanted them to be.

Consequently, every day when our birthday boy left for school, he found a new place to hide the blocks so they couldn't be messed with. But he didn't depend on that alone. He would also put me in charge of protecting them at all costs. Then, every day when he returned home from school, he checked on those blocks to be sure they were just as he had left them.

My son arranged his building blocks in a specific way. He knew what they were meant to form, and he didn't want them to be anything other than what he had created them to be. We too have been designed in a specific way with specific purposes. We were created in the image of God (see Gen. 1:26–27).

This week, we've studied how God exists in community: three persons in One. The fact that God exists in community means that we too were created for community. Yesterday, we learned that oneness in the body of Christ has a purpose. Let's read John 17:23 again, this time from the Amplified Bible:

> I in them and You in Me, that they may be perfected and completed into one, so that the world may know [without any doubt] that You sent Me, and [that You] have loved them, just as You have loved Me.

Why did Jesus pray for His disciples to be "perfected and completed into one"?

Now read Ephesians 3:10–11:

> God's purpose in all this was to use the church to display his wisdom in its rich variety to all the unseen rulers and authorities in the heavenly places. This was his eternal plan, which he carried out through Christ Jesus our Lord. (NLT)

According to these verses, what is God's purpose for His church?

What kind of plan does verse 11 say this was?

Before we go on, let me clarify that *church* and *body of Christ* are, for the most part, interchangeable terms. In this case, when Paul refers to God's purpose for the church, He is simultaneously talking about the body. When we consider the purposes God has in mind for His body, the oneness He calls us to in the body becomes much more pressing.

One scholar captured the weight of the purpose of the body of Christ when he said, "'It is through the church that Christ continues to accomplish the final purpose for which He assumed human nature.' ... The Church is, in this sense, the ongoing arena for the activity of God on earth."[1]

Oneness in the body impacts our one faith and mission to the world. As one body, we are called to contend both *for* something and *against* someone.

DIGGING IN

Read Jude 1:1–3:

> Jude, a servant of Jesus Christ and brother of James,
>
> To those who are called, beloved in God the Father and kept for Jesus Christ:
>
> May mercy, peace, and love be multiplied to you.
>
> Beloved, although I was very eager to write to you about our common salvation, I found it necessary to write appealing to you to contend for the faith that was once for all delivered to the saints.

Who is the writer of the letter?

To whom is he writing?

What did Jude want to write about?

What did he determine was necessary to write to them about?

The book of Jude is only one chapter long, and we don't have to read past the third verse to know the purpose of the letter. Jude wrote to fellow followers of Jesus to urge them to struggle for something worth fighting for. While he wanted to write to them about matters of salvation, Jude felt compelled to appeal to them to contend for the faith.

This is the same faith Paul spoke of in Ephesians 4. The Greek word Jude used for "contend" is *epagōnizomai*. It is used only here in all of Scripture, and it comes from the root word *agōnizomai*, an athletic term that refers to ancient Greek contests.[2] (Do you see the word *agony* in it?) This paints the picture of hard work that would be continuous, costly, and agonizing. While this may not seem like a pleasant idea, you probably practice contending more than you realize.

To help you identify things in your life you contend for, consider the following:

- When we own something, we watch over it and care for it. When problems or opponents come against what we feel like belongs to us, we confront them.
- When we believe that the outcome of a situation will impact our future, and when we agree that our actions can influence that impact, we contend.
- If we consider something to be of little value, we are less likely to sacrifice for it, but we fight for the things we hold most dear.

With these definitions in mind, what are some things you contend for?

What would it look like for you to contend for the faith?

Contending for the faith as one body in Christ becomes urgent when we understand that to contend *for* something means there is something to contend *against*. Our common faith comes with a *common enemy*. The early Christians who received Jude's message needed to contend for the faith for two reasons. First, because the message of salvation through Jesus had been entrusted to them (see v. 3), and second, because distorters of the faith were among them (see vv. 4–19).

In His last words before He went to the cross, Jesus also spoke about the common enemy of His followers. Read John 17:14–15:

> I have given them your word, and the world has hated them because they
> are not of the world, just as I am not of the world. I do not ask that you take
> them out of the world, but that you keep them from the evil one.

In this passage, Jesus identifies not one but two enemies. The first enemy Jesus speaks of is the world. This isn't the first time Jesus mentioned the world's hatred of His disciples. Two chapters earlier, Jesus had revealed to His disciples that because they belonged to Him, there would be places where they *didn't* belong (see John 15:18–25).

The second enemy Jesus points out is the Evil One. Paul also wrote about this enemy in his letter to the Ephesians. Look up and read Ephesians 6:10–20.

In the verses you just read, Paul attributes two specific tactics to the Devil (also known as *the Evil One*). What are they? (See vv. 11 and 16.)

Paul's goal for the follower of Jesus was to be able to stand firm against the tactics of the Evil One. How does he say we are to do that? (See vv. 11 and 13.)

In this passage, Paul names six pieces of the armor of God that the believer is to "take up" (v. 13). I want to focus on one, the shield of faith. We've already read how Paul identified himself as a "prisoner for the Lord" (see 4:1), and many scholars place this imprisonment as Paul's time in house arrest in Rome. If so, then Paul was likely writing this while looking at—or possibly even chained to—a Roman soldier.[3]

A Roman soldier would have two options for a shield. One would have been a smaller, circular shield used in hand-to-hand combat. The other option was larger and shaped more like a door. This shield was not designed to be used in individual hand-to-hand combat. Instead, it was most effective when used in tandem with other soldiers to create a shield wall. It is this shield that Paul referenced when he instructed believers to "take up the shield of faith."[4]

You're never safer separate.

Roman soldiers would use these door-shaped shields for both defense and offense. To defend against literal flaming darts flung by an enemy, Roman soldiers would dip their shields in water and position them to form an enclosure around themselves. The formation created the look of a turtle shell, which guarded them and extinguished the incoming fiery darts.[5] To advance, Roman soldiers stood side by side and linked their shields. With the strength and protection of the wall formed by their shields, Roman soldiers could advance together against their enemy, one step at a time.[6]

It was this image that Paul had in mind when he told the Ephesians to "take up the shield of faith, with which you can extinguish all the flaming darts of the evil one" (6:16). This shield of faith was not designed to be used alone. Together, we take up the shield of faith so that we may stand against our common enemy.

Satan tricks us into believing that the very place where we are safest is the place we should avoid, run from, or remove from our lives altogether. The truth is, you're never safer separate. Belonging binds us together as one. Together, we contend for our common faith. Together, we contend against our common enemies.

WORK IT OUT

The way we contend together is far different from the way the world fights. Look at the chart below, and contrast the differences between what the world says to contend for and how God's Word instructs us to contend.

THE WORLD	THE WORD	FOR FURTHER STUDY
Indulge in the moment	Be attentive and alert	Heb. 2:1; Eph. 6:18
Tear others down	Build each other up	Jude 1:20; Eph. 4:16
Pave your own way	Keep yourself in God's love	Jude 1:21; Eph. 4:2
Earn forgiveness	Forgive freely	Matt. 18:22; Eph. 4:32

In what ways are you fighting like the world instead of contending for the faith according to God's Word?

In the circumstances where you find yourself fighting like the world fights, how is it impacting your relationships with other followers of Jesus ... or distancing you from them altogether?

Day 4

What If I Get Hurt?

Memory Verse

Holy Father, keep them in _____ _____, which you have

_____ me, that _____ may be _____,

even as _____ are _____.

John 17:11b

A special note from Katy: *Before you begin today's study, it's important for you to know that there is a difference between common conflicts, which are sure to arise in the body of Christ, and church trauma or abuse. This study is not meant to address trauma or abuse. If you believe you have experienced church trauma or abuse, I encourage you to seek out a qualified Christian counselor.*

I wasn't going. No way, no how.

No matter how bad it hurt or how much he urged me, I absolutely was not going to the doctor to find out what was wrong. Weeks, maybe months, earlier, I had slipped and landed on my shoulder. Sure, it didn't feel good, but I didn't think much about it. I figured it out, kept going, and tried to make up for the minutes that had been lost.

In the days that followed, my shoulder felt tender, and there were certain movements I couldn't do without pain. Rather than addressing the issue, I opted to adjust. And when I couldn't move my arm in a certain direction, I simply used the other arm to accomplish whatever needed to be done.

After months like this, my husband finally refused to let it go on any longer. He scheduled an appointment for me to see a doctor, and I reluctantly went. First, the doctor put me through a series of movements with my healthy shoulder. I raised my left arm and folded it behind my head, then I extended that arm and wrapped it around my right shoulder. Each time, the doctor noted how far down my back my left hand could reach.

Then he had me repeat the same motions with my right shoulder. This time was different. The motions were tedious and painful, and the results caught my attention. In my determination to keep going, I had no idea how much I had lost.

After more tests, the doctor diagnosed me with a torn labrum. He prescribed intensive rehab and physical therapy to help me regain what I had lost over the weeks and months of ignoring my injury.

When I tore my labrum, the simplest solution seemed to be to ignore the pain and keep going. There were errands to run, laundry to fold, children to love, and a pace of life that wouldn't stop for a hurt shoulder. Yet ignoring the problem didn't heal my wound. It only made it worse.

Just like my shoulder, there will be pain in the body of Christ. Because we are all sinners and will not be made perfectly whole until we exit this life and join Jesus in eternity, we can expect that we will at times hurt one another. We may accidentally step on each other's toes, or we may intentionally wound one another.

Sometimes, it seems easier to ignore these offenses in the name of moving on and keeping the peace. I learned, though, there is danger in ignoring a problem in the body.

Read John 17:11 again:

> I am no longer in the world, but they are in the world, and I am coming to you. Holy Father, keep them in your name, which you have given me, that they may be one, even as we are one.

So far this week, we've discussed the phrase "that they may be one, even as we are one." Today, I want to talk about another part of this verse. Jesus makes a request to His Holy Father that His disciples would be one even as He and His Father are one.

What was Jesus' request?

The Greek word translated "keep" in this verse is *tēreō*, and it means "to attend to carefully, take care of, to guard."[1] It is the same word Jesus used in verse 15 when He asked God to "keep them from the evil one."

Paul also used this word in Ephesians 4:3 when he urged us to be "eager to maintain the unity of the Spirit in the bond of peace." But here's the thing: because oneness doesn't equal sameness, our distinctness can lead to conflict.

Yesterday, we learned about a common enemy we share as members of the body of Christ. Sometimes, the actions of other members of the body can make you feel like they are your enemy. When conflicts arise, we may not be so eager to guard the unity of the Spirit. But conflict doesn't have to separate us. Conflict can actually bring us closer. There is a difference between our common enemy and an offender in the body of Christ. Let's distinguish the two.

DIGGING IN

Read Acts 9:26–28:

> When he [Paul] had come to Jerusalem, he attempted to join the disciples. And they were all afraid of him, for they did not believe that he was a disciple. But Barnabas took him and brought him to the apostles and declared to them how on the road he had seen the Lord, who spoke to him, and how

at Damascus he had preached boldly in the name of Jesus. So he went in and out among them at Jerusalem, preaching boldly in the name of the Lord.

When Paul—the same Paul who authored the letter to the Ephesians—tried to join the disciples in Jerusalem, they still believed him to be an enemy of Jesus. Barnabas, however, vouched for Paul. He came alongside him and told the disciples about Paul's conversion and allegiance to Christ.

These verses mark the beginning of the powerful story of Paul and Barnabas. A few chapters later, we read that while they were worshipping and fasting with believers in the church at Antioch, "the Holy Spirit said, 'Set apart for me Barnabas and Saul for the work to which I have called them.' Then after fasting and praying they laid their hands on them and sent them off" (13:2–3).

Acts 13 marks the first time a church sent out missionaries to carry the gospel to other geographic locations. Before this moment, the good news of Jesus had spread as a result of persecution (see 11:19). The Holy Spirit set Paul and Barnabas apart, and the church in Antioch sent them out. The map below details their journey together.

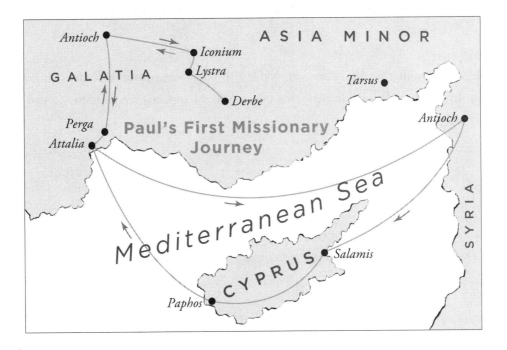

Researchers estimate their trip took at least two years and spanned more than twelve hundred miles. They traveled across land and water, visited nine cities, and established more than a dozen congregations.[2]

Their mission didn't come without opposition, though. Read the passages in the chart below, and record some of the details of what Paul and Barnabas faced together.

SCRIPTURE	LOCATION	EVENT	OUTCOME
Acts 13:6–12			
Acts 14:8–18			
Acts 14:19–20			

This first missionary journey was quite an adventure for Paul and Barnabas. Whether they were rejoicing over those who had believed in Jesus or fleeing angry mobs who sought to mistreat them, this great missionary pair strove side by side for the sake of the gospel. This first journey concludes at the end of chapter 14, when Paul and Barnabas gathered with the members of the church that had sent them out and reported all that God had done.

Think of a time in your life when you walked through something difficult with another person. In the space below, describe that event. What happened, and whom did you walk with through it?

What words would you use to describe the relationship between you and the person or people you walked with through that situation?

Together, Paul and Barnabas carried the message of Jesus to a world that had never heard it. They surely rejoiced together when people believed, and I can only assume they encouraged each other when it felt like no one responded to their message. They fled together at the threat of persecution, and Barnabas stayed by Paul's side after he endured stoning. Paul and Barnabas had gone through so much together. However, the next chapter tells us something surprising.

Read Acts 15:36–40:

> After some days Paul said to Barnabas, "Let us return and visit the brothers in every city where we proclaimed the word of the Lord, and see how they are." Now Barnabas wanted to take with them John called Mark. But Paul thought best not to take with them one who had withdrawn from them in Pamphylia and had not gone with them to the work. And there arose a sharp disagreement, so that they separated from each other. Barnabas took Mark with him and sailed away to Cyprus, but Paul chose Silas and departed, having been commended by the brothers to the grace of the Lord.

What did Paul and Barnabas disagree about?

Why didn't Paul want to take John Mark with them?

How did they resolve the conflict?

Paul and Barnabas encountered conflict—not from those who opposed their message but from each other. Conflict so strong, in fact, that it led them to separate.

Paul and Barnabas couldn't agree on whether to bring John Mark with them on their next missionary journey. Barnabas wanted to bring him; Paul did not.

On the first journey, John Mark had left Paul and Barnabas and returned home (see 13:13). As the men made plans for their next trip, it seems Barnabas wanted to give John Mark a second chance, but Paul didn't want to risk his deserting them again. Their conflicting opinions resulted in a sharp disagreement that eventually led them to separate from each other. Barnabas went one way with John Mark, and Paul went another way with Silas.

Put yourself in Paul and Barnabas' place. Imagine how you would feel if you disagreed to the point of parting ways with a person you'd walked through the storms of life with.

Describe some of those feelings in the space below.

I can't imagine what Paul and Barnabas must have felt in their moment of conflict. Surely, they each felt misunderstood, maybe even betrayed, by the other. They were probably frustrated and possibly angry. Yet the outcome of their disagreement didn't destroy their mission or message. Instead, it multiplied the reach of the gospel.

We can learn a few things from the sharp disagreement between Paul and Barnabas. First, Paul and Barnabas were two men who loved God. They believed in Jesus and risked their lives as they lived on mission for Him. Yet they still disagreed ... sharply.

Our love for Jesus will not insulate us from conflict with one another. This same Paul who could not come to common ground with his fellow partner on the mission field still championed oneness in the body of Christ and humility, gentleness, and love toward one another. What this tells me is that even when we disagree, we can still treat each other in a godly way.

Second, in spite of the conflict, the verses that detail their disagreement close with the phrase "having been commended by the brothers to the grace of the Lord" (15:40). While Paul and Barnabas couldn't agree on the right decision on the matter at hand, they could still agree on the grace of the Lord and the mission they had because of it. One writer observes, "The separation of Paul and Barnabas was a cooperative action, not a competitive one."[3]

Because we all love a happy ending, let's read a verse Paul wrote in a letter to Timothy several years after this conflict: "Luke alone is with me. Get Mark and bring him with you, for he is very useful to me for ministry" (2 Tim. 4:11). This Mark, whom Paul asked for and called "useful" to his ministry, is the same John Mark from Acts 15. The sharp disagreement between Paul and Barnabas had ended in reconciliation and continued cooperation to share the message of Jesus.

Jesus also understood feelings of rejection, misunderstanding, betrayal, and disappointment. Yet He still pursued His disciples and prayed for them to be one. As we close today's study, let's go to a tender moment between Jesus and one of His closest disciples on earth.

Read Luke 22:31–34:

> "Simon, Simon, behold, Satan demanded to have you, that he might sift you like wheat, but I have prayed for you that your faith may not fail. And when you have turned again, strengthen your brothers." Peter said to him, "Lord, I am ready to go with you both to prison and to death." Jesus said, "I tell you, Peter, the rooster will not crow this day, until you deny three times that you know me."

Jesus knew what would unfold within hours after speaking with Peter. Despite all they had been through together—the miracles Peter had witnessed, the teaching he had heard, the faithfulness he had seen, the love of Jesus he had experienced—during Jesus' most difficult moments on earth, Peter would deny and desert His Lord. It's hard to even describe the feelings that would be associated with such betrayal. Yet Jesus gave us an example to follow.

Knowing full well what would soon transpire between Himself and His disciples, Jesus planned to forgive. He prayed for Peter and instructed Him what to do when he "turned again."

The Bible records what happened after Jesus' prediction about Peter came to pass. When Jesus had endured the cross and conquered the grave, He showed the forgiveness that He'd already planned to extend. In the last chapter of his gospel, John records how the resurrected

Jesus sat with Peter at daybreak on the shore of a sea. Jesus ended His conversation with Peter with the same words He began with: "Follow me."[4]

Jesus gave us the example of forgiveness planned and forgiveness shown. In the body of Christ, we cannot expect to live free from conflict, but we can choose to follow Jesus each day. This cannot be done apart from the work of the Holy Spirit in and through us, but as we unite in one faith, one Spirit, one Lord, and one God and Father, we can surrender to His will and choose forgiveness planned and forgiveness shown.

Jesus gave us the example of forgiveness planned and forgiveness shown.

WORK IT OUT

As we seek to apply what we've learned today, I want to discuss both the gift of conflict and the risk of conflict.

I know we don't often connect the word *gift* to the idea of conflict. However, conflict can be a gift because it can create opportunity for response and reconciliation.

In my own life, I can recall a specific time when a friend I had wronged brought it to my attention. I'd had no idea I had hurt her. When she chose to confront my offense instead of ignoring the pain and not addressing it, she afforded me the opportunity to apologize and ask for her forgiveness. We confront because we care, not because we must be right or get our way (which we'll talk more about in week 4) but because we care about Christ, His mission, and His body.

Is God putting someone on your heart right now whom you could bless with the gift of confronting a wrong and seeking reconciliation? Who is it, and what is the situation?

To be fair, I should say that not everyone will consider your gift of confrontation a blessing. With the gift of conflict admittedly comes the risk of conflict. We risk being rejected, misunderstood, or dismissed. But when the goal of conflict is oneness in the body of Christ, the reward far outweighs the risk associated with maintaining unity in the body.

To help you approach conflict in the body of Christ with a heart that honors God and seeks His glory, here are three questions to ask yourself when you encounter conflict with a member of the body of Christ:

- What about this is between God and me?
- What about this is between God and them?
- What needs to happen between them and me in order to glorify God?

Day 5

Do It Together: Pray

Memory Verse

Holy Father, keep them in _____ _____, *which you have*

you have _____ *me, that* _____ *may be*

_____, *even as* _____ *are* _____.

John 17:11b

As I settled into a new neighborhood and new routines, I felt overwhelmed and alone. I had six small children who depended on me for everything and no one around to help me. I knew God's promises about how He'd never leave me, but I still woke up each day afraid.

In one desperate moment, I prayed, "God, please tell someone to pray for me. Put me on someone's heart. Tell them I need them to intercede for me."

Months later, I passed by a new friend. I had met her around the same time I was struggling through each day. We'd never really hung out, and our conversations were usually short, but she was a sweet friend, and I always enjoyed bumping into her.

This particular day, I could tell she was nervous as she said, "I didn't know whether to tell you this." She went on to tell me how several months earlier, after the very first day we'd met, God had put me on her heart and she'd begun praying for me regularly.

As I remember it, my jaw dropped, and I could barely form words to respond to her. When I'd begged God to put me on someone's heart, I'd imagined the people I knew. I never imagined that an acquaintance I barely knew, one who didn't even know what to pray for me, would be the one God would choose to be the answer to my prayer.

This week, we've studied some of Jesus' last words before He went to the cross. What we've discovered is that in the shadow of being betrayed, denied, and deserted by those who walked closest to Him on earth, Jesus prayed for them. We also read yesterday about how Jesus prayed specifically for Peter and the circumstances he would encounter.

Praying *for* one another and *with* one another is a privilege and a blessing to be shared with the members of the body of Christ. Below are some examples of what the Bible says about praying with one other and for one another:

We can pray with one mind and purpose.
- All these with one accord were devoting themselves to prayer, together with the women and Mary the mother of Jesus, and his brothers. (Acts 1:14)
- They devoted themselves to the apostles' teaching and the fellowship, to the breaking of bread and the prayers. (Acts 2:42)

We can join each other's struggles through prayer.
- I urge you, brothers and sisters, by our Lord Jesus Christ and by the love of the Spirit, to join me in my struggle by praying to God for me. (Rom. 15:30 NIV)
- Peter was kept in prison, but earnest prayer for him was made to God by the church. (Acts 12:5)

We can persevere together in prayer.
- With all prayer and petition pray [with specific requests] at all times [on every occasion and in every season] in the Spirit, and with this in view, stay alert with all perseverance and petition [interceding in prayer] for all God's people. (Eph. 6:18 AMP)
- Be joyful in hope, patient in affliction, faithful in prayer. (Rom. 12:12 NIV)

When we pray *with* one another and *for* one another, our faith grows, our burdens are shared, and our unity is displayed.

We don't have to reserve prayer for one day a week. We don't have to limit our prayers to our closest friends or family. We don't have to bear our burdens alone. Because we belong to Jesus and are members of His body, we can pray with each other and for each other at all times and about all things.

WORK IT OUT

Use the space below to reflect on the things we've discussed this week. Consider the following:

What situations or conflicts am I facing right now? (Ask God to reveal to you how to handle them in a way that will seek to maintain unity in the body of Christ and glorify Him.)

What have I learned this week that has changed how I approach oneness in the body of Christ?

Who is one person I can pray for today whom I may not talk to or spend time with often but whom I share the common bond of Jesus with and can strive together with in prayer?

Thank God for the privilege and blessing of coming to Him in prayer together with other believers, and ask Him to help you remain faithful and persistent in prayer.

Seven Scriptures to Help You Navigate Conflict in the Body of Christ

If it is possible, as far as it depends on you, live at peace with everyone. (Rom. 12:18 NIV)

Good sense and discretion make a man slow to anger, and it is his honor and glory to overlook a transgression or an offense [without seeking revenge and harboring resentment]. (Prov. 19:11 AMP)

Understand this, my beloved brothers and sisters. Let everyone be quick to hear [be a careful, thoughtful listener], slow to speak [a speaker of carefully chosen words and], slow to anger [patient, reflective, forgiving]. (James 1:19 AMP)

With the tongue we praise our Lord and Father, and with it we curse human beings, who have been made in God's likeness. Out of the same mouth come praise and cursing. My brothers and sisters, this should not be. (James 3:9–10 NIV)

Where jealousy and selfish ambition exist, there will be disorder and every vile practice. But the wisdom from above is first pure, then peaceable, gentle, open to reason, full of mercy and good fruits, impartial and sincere. (James 3:16–17)

If another believer sins against you, go privately and point out the offense. If the other person listens and confesses it, you have won that person back. (Matt. 18:15 NLT)

Then Peter came to him and asked, "Lord, how often should I forgive someone who sins against me? Seven times?" "No, not seven times," Jesus replied, "but seventy times seven!" (Matt. 18:21–22 NLT)

Week 2 Group Time

Welcome

- Leader: Introduce week 2 by asking each member to share anything she underlined or highlighted throughout the week's study.
- Review the memory verse for the week: John 17:11b.

Watch the week 2 video: "You Belong Here."

Discussion Questions

- Belonging brings oneness. How do you define *oneness*?
- Read Matthew 10:1–4. What differences do you see in Jesus' disciples? What united them in spite of their differences?
- Read John 17:20–23. What was on Jesus' mind just before He died on the cross? How does that impact your thoughts about being one in the body of Christ?
- Read the bullet points on day 3 that help you identify things in your life you contend for. With those definitions in mind, what do you contend for? What would it look like to contend for the faith?
- Katy wrote, "Conflict doesn't have to separate us. Conflict can actually bring us closer." How does the example of Paul and Barnabas change your perspective on conflict in the body of Christ?
- Read the verses about prayer on day 5.

Close in Prayer

- Ask for prayer requests; then pray. Thank God for the privilege of coming to Him in prayer *together*.
- Ask God to help you stop pulling your own way and instead pull together for the cause of Christ.

Week 3

The Key to Keeping It Together

Memory Verse

Make every effort to keep the oneness of the Spirit in the bond of peace [each individual working together to make the whole successful].

Ephesians 4:3 AMP

Introduction

This wasn't what I remembered. Instead of feeling thrilled, I prayed for it all to be over.

On what I had expected would be a fun family vacation, my family and I made our way to a theme park. We had planned this trip for months and looked forward to the many attractions we'd experience. We'd made lists of the things we didn't want to miss and ordered each day to make sure we did everything on the list. My husband and I had visited this park before, so we pointed our children to the rides and attractions we thought they would enjoy.

The day started out fine. We rode roller coasters and simulators. No one got sick, and no one got scared. That's when we came to this particular ride ... which in my head I had remembered as fun. It was a ride I had looked forward to experiencing with my children. As our moment to board approached, we walked in, took our seats, and fastened our seatbelts. Up to this point, everything felt normal and was exactly what I had expected.

The ride started. We wove through darkness ... not my favorite but still what I remembered and expected. We arrived at the moment when we did what felt like a freefall from way up high in the sky. Again, something I remembered and expected.

What I didn't recall, however, was how loose the seatbelt felt as we plummeted toward the ground. Enter fear, terror, eyes clenched closed, and prayer. Lots of prayer.

I opened my eyes long enough to find something to hold on to. When I saw a metal bar in front of me, I reached out, grabbed it, and held on as tightly as my hands could squeeze it. I clenched my eyes shut again and began to pray, "God, please let this ride end. Please let it be over. Please get us off this ride. Please let no one fly out."

Up and down we went. With each drop, my bottom came up out of my seat. Yes, the seatbelt kept me from flying out of the roller coaster car, but it wasn't tight enough for me to enjoy the ride. Since my bottom came out of my seat, I assumed everyone else's bottoms were doing the same. I had one of my sons within reach, so I grabbed his hand and squeezed it between my hand and the bar to which that hand clung so tightly.

When the ride finally ended, I wiped the sweat from my brow and took a few deep breaths to slow down my heart rate. While my son rubbed his squashed hand, I announced that I would never ride that ride again. Never. Ever. Again.

Day 1

When You Feel Like You're Falling Apart

Memory Verse

Make every effort to keep the oneness of the Spirit in the bond of peace [each individual working together to make the whole successful].

Ephesians 4:3 AMP

After declaring I would never ride that ride again—*ever* again—I wondered why I had even gotten on it in the first place. I had ridden this ride years before. I was at least a little familiar with what would happen once I boarded. Something about the first time had been different, though. I didn't recall feeling such terror. I'd enjoyed it enough to get back on it a second time and even bring my kids aboard. What on earth could have been so different the first time?

It wasn't until I viewed the photos they take of your screaming family on the ride that I realized the difference maker. In the photo, there I was with my eyes squinted shut, gripping my son's hand and the bar in front of me. A few seats over, there were my daughters on either side of my husband, holding tightly to their daddy's strong arms. That was the difference.

The first time around, we hadn't had our kids on the ride with us. *I* sat next to my husband, and *I* held on to his big, strong arm. Holding so tightly to something that felt secure changed my experience. Instead of dreadful fear, I enjoyed the ride and even boarded it a second time with my kids. The key was having a secure structure to cling to … something that didn't threaten to fall apart.

What are you trying to keep together right now that feels dangerously close to falling apart?

Whether it's a calendar you're juggling, a situation at work that hangs in the balance, your marriage, or another relationship, when the pieces of your life feel like they're falling apart, that anxiety reaches into every other part of your life.

When we find ourselves in the middle of these messes, we often revert to my mantra on the ski slope that day. (See the introduction "I've Got This.") We try to figure it out, catch up where we feel like we're falling behind, or just keep going. But the truth is that none of those options really solve anything when the fibers of our lives start to unravel.

And they will unravel. At some point, and probably more than one point in our lives, circumstances will cause us to feel like everything is falling apart. While this doesn't sound promising, and maybe you're wondering what in the world it could possibly have to do with belonging, there is very good news.

The wholeness of Christ holds us together, even when life falls apart.

Read Ephesians 4:1–3:

> I therefore, a prisoner for the Lord, urge you to walk in a manner worthy of
> the calling to which you have been called, with all humility and gentleness,
> with patience, bearing with one another in love, eager to maintain the unity
> of the Spirit in the bond of peace.

In week 1, we studied the calling to which we have been called. In the verses above, Paul lists four practical ways to do this. Today, I want to focus on the last phrase of these verses: "eager to maintain the unity of the Spirit in the bond of peace."

What would it take for you to feel that you have peace in your life and circumstances?

Maybe you feel you'd have peace if you could just figure out how to fix a problem. You may feel like you'd live in peace if everyone would just do what you ask them. You may have even said you'd have peace if people would leave you alone.

On the surface, the qualities of humility, gentleness, patience, and bearing with each other in love don't seem to go together with peace. The need for patience or bearing with someone often means something isn't moving as quickly as you'd like or someone isn't responding as you'd like them to. Typically, when things don't go our way, we don't expect to find peace around the next corner.

The Greek word translated "bond of peace" is *eirēnē* (eye-RAY-nay). While it's likely you don't speak Greek and will probably never have much of a reason to do so, I included the phonetic spelling because I hope that by the end of today's study, this will be a word you'll want to think about, talk about, and remember often. So before you go any further, I want you to attempt to say this word out loud.

eye—like your eyeball
ray—like a ray of sunshine
nay—like the sound a horse makes

How'd it go? Do you speak Greek now? Great, let's keep moving.

Scholars believe *eirēnē* comes from the root word *eirō*, which means "to join, tie together into a whole." It can further be defined as "properly, wholeness, i.e., when all essential parts are joined together; *peace* (God's gift of wholeness)."[1]

In the introduction of our study, we talked about the frustrations of putting a puzzle together only to find a piece missing. So far, we've found our missing piece—the community that comes with our calling. Today, we will learn about something that acts like puzzle glue.

I remember when I discovered puzzle glue during my preteen years. I was elated. I didn't know you could put a puzzle together and never have to worry about it falling apart. Puzzle glue provided me with so many options for what I could do with my completed puzzles. I chose puzzles I thought my friends would like, put them together, glued them together, then framed them and gave them away as gifts.

That's what *eiréné* does for us in the body of Christ. It's not just a peace (not to be confused with *piece*) in which the waves of life are calm for only the moment. It's so much more than that. It's a peace that creates completeness no matter what we face. It's a wholeness that holds together in the midst of suffering and disappointment. This peace is God's gift of wholeness.

Read Ephesians 2:14, 16:

> He himself is our peace, who has made us both one and has broken down in
> his flesh the dividing wall of hostility … and might reconcile us both to God
> in one body through the cross, thereby killing the hostility.

Who is our peace?

How did Jesus reconcile us to God?

What did we become because of His death on the cross?

Because we belong to Jesus, we have a *common bond*, the bond of peace. The problem, though, is that we don't always hold on. When life becomes fragile and the pieces start to shake, we pull away from each other. Our common enemy tells us no one thinks or cares about us, and we wonder if anyone would even notice if they never heard from us again. It feels safer to hide from others.

But today, I want to give you another option. When life feels like it's falling apart, we can press into the body of Christ instead of pulling away from it. The key to keeping it together is coming together. Let's learn more about this common bond of peace.

DIGGING IN

Chapters 14–17 in the gospel of John are often referred to as Jesus' farewell address. These four chapters chronicle the time between Jesus partaking of the Lord's Supper with His disciples in the upper room (chapter 13) and the betrayal and arrest that eventually led to His crucifixion (chapter 18). During this intimate exchange—His final words to His disciples—Jesus twice tells them about His peace.

First, in 14:27 Jesus says, "Peace I leave with you; my peace I give to you. Not as the world gives do I give to you. Let not your hearts be troubled, neither let them be afraid."

What does Jesus say He is leaving with His disciples?

Jesus makes an important distinction about the peace He gives. Where does Jesus say this peace will *not* be found?

What can the disciples do (or not do) because of the peace Jesus leaves with them?

Later in this same discussion, Jesus returns to the point: "I have said these things to you, that in me you may have peace. In the world you will have tribulation. But take heart; I have overcome the world" (16:33). Twice before He died for the sins of the world, Jesus told His disciples about the peace they could find only in Him.

Then, in His very first words to His disciples after His resurrection, Jesus pointed to this same peace again.

Read John 20:19–21:

> On the evening of that day, the first day of the week, the doors being locked where the disciples were for fear of the Jews, Jesus came and stood among them and said to them, "Peace be with you." When he had said this, he showed them his hands and his side. Then the disciples were glad when they saw the Lord. Jesus said to them again, "Peace be with you. As the Father has sent me, even so I am sending you."

Go back and read verses 1–10. What significant event happened early on the day the disciples were gathered behind locked doors?

According to verse 19, Jesus came and did what?

What did He say as He stood among the disciples?

Eight days later a similar scene unfolded. Read verses 26–28:

> Eight days later, his disciples were inside again, and Thomas was with them. Although the doors were locked, Jesus came and stood among them and said, "Peace be with you." Then he said to Thomas, "Put your finger here, and see my hands; and put out your hand, and place it in my side. Do not disbelieve, but believe." Thomas answered him, "My Lord and my God!"

I love the exclamation point at the end of Thomas' answer. Jesus showed Him the scars left by the crucifixion, and Thomas believed. Jesus' scars served as proof of His victory over sin and death. His scars act as the bridge to peace and belonging that can be found only in Him and in His body.

When the world falls apart, Jesus—and the bond of peace in His body—holds us together.

WORK IT OUT

Up to this point in our study, we've talked about the body of Christ and how your quest for belonging is directly tied to responding to your calling and receiving your community in the body.

As we continue our study, though, you will begin to see that the body of Christ is not only an essential piece of *your* belonging but that *you* are an essential part of the body of Christ. You're not whole without them, but neither are they whole without you. Part of the definition of *eirēnē* includes the phrase "when all essential parts are joined together." As a member of the body of Christ, the whole body benefits when you take your place in it.

Do you believe that? If not, what keeps you from believing you are an essential part of the body of Christ? Use the space below to write an honest prayer to God. Tell Him how you feel and the places in your heart that make you want to pull away instead of press into the body of Christ. Ask Him to answer your fears, your hurts, or the places that are falling apart in your life with His truth.

You're not whole without them, but neither are they whole without you.

Day 2

Following the Steps of Wholeness

Memory Verse

Make every effort to _____ the

_____ of the Spirit in the bond of peace [each

individual working together to make the whole successful].

Ephesians 4:3 AMP

I'm sure it was supposed to be fun ... even magical ... yet the only thing I felt was dread.

With the sounds, scents, and festivities of the Christmas season surrounding us, my daughter couldn't wait to build a gingerbread house. She'd received a kit as a gift, and each day after school she asked with an eager heart, "Can we build the gingerbread house today?"

For several days, we'd had other after-school activities to attend, but on this day, I no longer had an excuse. Today would be the day we built the gingerbread house, and I fully expected today to also be the day the gingerbread house fell apart. Because in my experience, that's exactly what would happen. In all my years of attempting to make gingerbread houses, I hadn't once—not one time—successfully built one that didn't fall apart almost immediately.

Nevertheless, here we were: me, my daughter, gingerbread walls, a gingerbread roof, and icing—a lot of icing.

I was determined that this time would be different.

We unfolded the directions and read them carefully. We didn't get in a rush. We used as much icing as we could squeeze out of the tube. I treated the icing like the glue it was supposed to be, and since I knew these things were likely to fall apart, we didn't hold back. "More icing!" I'd tell my daughter.

We raised the four walls into place and surveyed our project thus far. The walls appeared sturdy and secure. So far so good.

Following the directions' prompting, we then reached for the roof of the gingerbread house. We stayed with our "the more the merrier" approach with the icing-glue, but that's when our creation took a turn for the worse.

When we tried to join the roof to the walls, they started to slip out of place. They no longer held together at the peak, and one side of the roof began to slide down a wall. This was not at all like puzzle glue.

We tried to put the roof back together, pressing it into place and holding it for several minutes, but to no avail. That's when my daughter said, "It doesn't look like the one on the box."

Um, ya' think? To be honest, I hadn't known that's what we were going for.

The good news in this scenario, however, is that even if the gingerbread house falls apart, you still have lots of icing and candy. Whether the pieces are beautifully adhered together in a whole gingerbread house or falling off and scattered about, it all tastes the same. At least, that's what I told my daughter.

After our sad attempt at making a gingerbread house, our family took a Christmas vacation to one of our favorite places in the mountains. An activity they offered was none other than gingerbread house making. *Sigh.*

But this project was different. When we arrived to make the gingerbread houses, we found that the walls and roofs had already been prepared. All we had to do was use icing to decorate the house with candy. My eyes widened with glee over all the trouble we would not have to face.

I suspect they used a lot more than icing to keep those walls and roofs in place, because they didn't budge. They were stuck together good, and because we didn't have to worry about the whole thing falling apart, we had a marvelous time decorating our gingerbread houses. I actually smiled while working with gingerbread pieces! And I have memories of laughter and giggles and the whole family getting along. This time was much different than the first.

Read Ephesians 4:1–3 again:

> I therefore, a prisoner for the Lord, urge you to walk in a manner worthy of
> the calling to which you have been called, with all humility and gentleness,
> with patience, bearing with one another in love, eager to maintain the unity
> of the Spirit in the bond of peace.

So far in our study, we've discussed the calling to which we've been called and the oneness necessary to walk in a manner worthy of that calling. This week, we'll talk about how we can practically walk in oneness in the body of Christ and why it's so essential to belonging.

Verse 2 gives us four imperatives for *how* we walk in a manner worthy of our calling. List those four things in the space below:

What word connects *called* to the four imperatives you just listed?

These four things act as puzzle glue in the bond of peace. They are the steps that lead to wholeness, and Paul doesn't make them optional. Let's look at some other verses in Scripture to get a better understanding of these four words. Read the following verses, and underline or highlight the words that are also mentioned in Ephesians 4:2:

- The fruit of the Spirit is love, joy, peace, patience, kindness, goodness, faithfulness, gentleness, self-control; against such things there is no law. (Gal. 5:22–23)

- Take my yoke upon you. Let me teach you, because I [Jesus] am humble and gentle at heart, and you will find rest for your souls. (Matt. 11:29 NLT)

It's important to note how completely opposite these attitudes are from what we naturally produce in our flesh. These verses give us the source of the attitudes of love, patience, gentleness, and humility: it is only by Jesus and His Spirit that we can act in these ways.

This is a great time to recall that Jesus is the head of the body (see Eph. 4:15). It is only by abiding in Him that we can maintain unity in His body. The same way our identity *in* Christ leads to the body *of* Christ, our quest to belong in the body of Christ should always lead us to our head, Jesus.

If you're not already convinced that identity in Christ includes your participation in the body of Christ, this ought to seal the deal.

To walk in a manner worthy of our calling, we must walk with humility, gentleness, patience, and love. By definition, humility, gentleness, patience, and love simply cannot be practiced alone. They must be shown toward others, and they must be received from others.

Each of these words is relational. They are lived out within the body of Christ. They help us maintain the unity of the Spirit in the bond of peace. These actions are so essential to our unity in the body of Christ that in the final hours before His crucifixion, *these* were the things our Lord and head of the body, Jesus, talked about and demonstrated to His disciples.

DIGGING IN

Open your Bible to John 13, and read verses 1–11.

As this chapter begins, we find Jesus with His disciples at supper. This chapter directly precedes Jesus' farewell address, which we've discussed throughout our study.

Here, John makes a point to tell us a few things Jesus knew. List those in the space below. (See verses 1, 3.)

How does verse 1 describe Jesus' relationship with His disciples?

Read verses 4b–5:

> He laid aside his outer garments, and taking a towel, tied it around his waist.
> Then he poured water into a basin and began to wash the disciples' feet and
> to wipe them with the towel that was wrapped around him.

Maybe you've seen a painting that depicts Jesus with His disciples in the upper room that night. If you have, the picture in your mind is likely one of Jesus with His disciples gathered around a table. They're comfortable, they're eating, and they're together. Yet Jesus knew that the next several hours would hold the unraveling of His earthly existence. He would be arrested, tried, and crucified. His disciples would be scattered, confused, and dismayed.

It is in this context that Jesus left the place of fellowship at the table with His disciples and engaged in a series of actions recorded in verses 4–5. Jesus

- got up from the table,
- took off His outer garment,
- tied a towel around His waist,
- poured water into a large bowl, and
- began to wash the feet of His disciples.

The activity Jesus engaged in was not uncommon in their time and culture. Foot washing was necessary for several reasons, mainly because the shoe of the day was a sandal and the roads they traveled were dusty. They didn't have the shoe options we have today: closed toe, open toe, loafer, wedge, stiletto. No, they likely had one pair of sandals that exposed much of the foot. They also didn't have paved roads or sidewalks as we do today. Combine those elements and what you get is dirty, stinky feet. The surprise here isn't the foot washing; it's who was doing the foot washing.[1]

In most households, servants washed the feet of guests. The master of the house didn't do such an unpleasant task. Yet Jesus, the disciples' Lord and master, humbled Himself by taking the form of a servant and washing their feet. In the opening verses of Ephesians 4, the word Paul uses for humility is *tapeinophrosynē*, which means "'lowliness of mind,' the humble recognition of the worth and value of other people."[2]

In the hours before His death, as Jesus washed the feet of His disciples, He taught them humility and gentleness. He humbled Himself, taking a role and doing an activity they would have associated with a servant. So much so that Peter even tried to resist Jesus' humble demonstration (see v. 8a). In response to Peter's resistance, Jesus extended the call to humility and gentleness: "If I do not wash you, you have no share with me" (v. 8b).

But Jesus wasn't finished teaching. Later in this chapter, Jesus addressed the issue of bearing with one another in love.

Read verses 34–35:

> A new commandment I give to you, that you love one another: just as I have loved you, you also are to love one another. By this all people will know that you are my disciples, if you have love for one another.

What new commandment did Jesus give His disciples?

How does Jesus say people will know they are His disciples?

In a letter John wrote to doubting Christians several years after Jesus' death and resurrection, he took the call to love one step further. Read 1 John 2:9–11:

> Whoever says he is in the light and hates his brother is still in darkness. Whoever loves his brother abides in the light, and in him there is no cause for stumbling. But whoever hates his brother is in the darkness and walks in the darkness, and does not know where he is going, because the darkness has blinded his eyes.

What does John say is directly connected to walking in the light?

The Amplified Bible translates verse 1 John 2:10 like this: "The one who loves and unselfishly seeks the best for his [believing] brother lives in the Light, and in him there is no occasion for stumbling or offense [he does not hurt the cause of Christ or lead others to sin]."

Love is a thread that pulls through every part of the body of Christ, and the book of Ephesians has much to say about it. Look at the verses in the chart below, and connect them to what they say about love and the body of Christ.

Ephesians 3:17	We are to walk in love as Christ loved us.
Ephesians 4:15	We are to speak the truth to one another in love.
Ephesians 4:16	We can be rooted and grounded in Christ's love.
Ephesians 5:2	The body of Christ builds itself up in love.

Jesus is the light of the world (see John 8:12). To walk in the light, we must walk as Jesus walked, and that includes walking in humility, gentleness, patience, and love.

WORK IT OUT

Because we belong to Jesus, we have been given the common bond of peace with every member of His body. As we seek to maintain the bond of peace by practicing humility, gentleness, patience, and love, let's go back to Jesus' example of foot washing. Look back at the list of practical steps Jesus took to wash His disciples' feet.

To wash their feet, Jesus left His current place at the table. He took off something, and He also put on something. To engage in this act of humility and gentleness, Jesus also needed a few things, like water and a bowl.

With Jesus' example in mind, consider these questions:

To eagerly maintain the bond of peace, do I need to move from my physical position to actively demonstrate humility, gentleness, patience, or love? Or do I possibly need to move from my mental or emotional position on a matter?

To eagerly maintain the bond of peace, is there something I need to take off, like pride or bitterness?

To eagerly maintain the bond of peace, is there something I need to put on, like forgiveness or compassion?

What resources do I have at my disposal that I can use to eagerly maintain the bond of peace?

Day 3

The Enemy of Belonging

Memory Verse

Make every effort to _____ the _____
of the Spirit in the _____ of _____
[each individual working together to make the whole successful].
Ephesians 4:3 AMP

He was larger than life.

His chin always seemed to tilt toward the sky, and though he was much smaller than everyone else, he sauntered in and out of every room as though he were the most important one there. He wasn't known for being nice, but he was educated and talented. He got everything he wanted, even if he had to cheat and lie to get it. While he found himself in over his head at times, he always seemed to land on his feet.

This little mouse played one of the main characters in a kids' movie a few years ago, and I think he is a great illustration of what it looks like to do things our way. The world persuades us to prioritize our feelings and ask questions like "What makes me happy?" and "What do I want?" That way doesn't lead to belonging, according to God's Word.

Read Ephesians 4:3 from the Amplified Bible: "Make every effort to keep the oneness of the Spirit in the bond of peace [each individual working together to make the whole successful]."

Yesterday, using examples from Jesus, we learned how to make every effort to keep the oneness of the Spirit. We looked at how humility, gentleness, patience, and love help us work together to make the whole body successful. Today, let's talk about what it looks like when we *aren't* working together.

The opposite of a servant heart is a selfish heart. It's the difference between a *we* mindset and a *me* mindset. As long as I have *me* on my mind, the qualities listed in Ephesians 4 will be hard to find in my life. When we focus on ourselves, pride creeps in. As one scholar concludes, "Pride lurks behind all discord, while the greatest single secret of concord is humility."[1]

The world will tempt you to tie your peace to yourself—to what you can acquire, accomplish, or adventure. As we've discovered, though, the bond of peace in the body of Christ is far different from the peace the world offers. One changes with the winds of your circumstances; the other is from the One who is peace and never changes. Only the Prince of Peace can lead you to belonging.

It's important for us to be alert to the things that cause us to shift our mindset from *we* to *me*. God's Word warns us about pride and its destructive nature (see Matt. 23:12; James 4:7; 1 Pet. 5:6). In week 1 of our study, we took a trip back to the Old Testament to learn about the biblical concept of community in the nation of Israel. We talked about their exodus out of slavery in Egypt and how they were a community called to worship and witness. To help us identify pride and guard against it in our own lives, let's look at examples from the ruler of Egypt at the time when God miraculously delivered Israel.

DIGGING IN

Open your Bible and read Exodus 9:13–35. What does verse 17 say Pharaoh is still doing?

Through His servant Moses, God offered the ruler of Egypt multiple opportunities to let Israel go free. Time and time again, Pharaoh refused. Verse 17 records the reason: "You are still exalting yourself against my people and will not let them go."

Pharaoh's unwillingness to yield to God was rooted in his pride (see 10:3). The plagues recorded in Exodus 9–10, along with Pharaoh's prideful response to God, show us what to watch out for in our own lives and how to guard against pride and the destruction it brings.

First, we see that pride puts off full surrender. Read 9:18–21:

> Behold, about this time tomorrow I will cause very heavy hail to fall, such as never has been in Egypt from the day it was founded until now. Now therefore send, get your livestock and all that you have in the field into safe shelter, for every man and beast that is in the field and is not brought home will die when the hail falls on them." Then whoever feared the word of the LORD among the servants of Pharaoh hurried his slaves and his livestock into the houses, but whoever did not pay attention to the word of the LORD left his slaves and his livestock in the field.

Upon hearing God's words, what did some of Pharaoh's servants do?

Why did they hurry to move people and animals into safe shelter?

After hearing the threat of this severe plague, some in Pharaoh's court "feared the word of the LORD." That's certainly better than *not* fearing it or not heeding the warning. It shows a basic level of belief in the Lord. However, scholars point out the gap between fearing the *word* of the Lord and fearing the Lord. While they may have acknowledged God's power, they still lacked the repentance that would produce full surrender.[2]

Moses revealed their unchanged hearts just a few verses later. Because the hail had not taken *everything* from them, Pharaoh and his servants relied on what they had left and acted pridefully, refusing to fear the Lord (see vv. 30–32).

In week 2, we learned that belonging requires full surrender to the will of God. With Pharaoh as an example, we see that when we hold on to anything other than Jesus, we can be inclined to be prideful and act according to our own will in pursuit of our desires.

What might you be holding on to that is keeping you from experiencing true belonging and the bond of peace?

Second, pride pushes back against total obedience. Read Exodus 10:8–11:

> Moses and Aaron were brought back to Pharaoh. And he said to them, "Go, serve the LORD your God. But which ones are to go?" Moses said, "We will go with our young and our old. We will go with our sons and daughters and with our flocks and herds, for we must hold a feast to the LORD." But he said to them, "The LORD be with you, if ever I let you and your little ones go! Look, you have some evil purpose in mind. No! Go, the men among you, and serve the LORD, for that is what you are asking." And they were driven out from Pharaoh's presence.

After Pharaoh told Moses to go, what question did he ask?

Instead of completely obeying God, what did Pharaoh want to do?

For five chapters of the book of Exodus, Moses has been feeding Pharaoh the same line: "Let my people go." And for five chapters, Pharaoh has been responding with the answer: "No." Egypt has experienced plagues that turned the nation's water into blood and covered the land in frogs, gnats, and flies. Egyptian livestock and crops have died, and the Egyptian people and animals have been covered in sores. Here, in the face of yet another devastating plague, Pharaoh tries to make a deal. He wants to escape the consequences of continued disobedience to God, but he doesn't want to obey Him completely.

Have you ever tried to make a deal with God? Describe it in the space below.

Finally, pride ruins more than just one life. Immediately before these verses in Exodus 10, Pharaoh's servants pleaded with him to do what Moses asked. The question they posed to Pharaoh is heartbreaking: "Do you not yet understand that Egypt is ruined?" (v. 7). It seems Pharaoh's pride had blinded him to the reality that his land, his people, and his entire nation were destroyed.

It's not hard to recognize the disastrous impact of pride in Pharaoh's story. I doubt this is a path any one of us would willingly walk. However, pride does not always appear as obviously as it did in Pharaoh's life.

You may be able to trace your perceptions of pride all the way back to your grade-school playground. You may have noticed that the kids with the nicest shoes, greatest abilities, or best vacation stories were the ones everyone wanted to be around. It seems that even from an early age, life teaches us that the bigger and better your life appears, the more you will belong.

Because of this, the roots of pride may actually grow out of your desire to belong—or at least the desire to avoid the sting of not belonging. However, according to God's Word, this is a backward approach to belonging. When we act in pride, we're willing to share only our strengths. True humility, though, frees us to share our struggles.

The author of the letter to the Ephesians understood this well. Paul had a long list of strengths in his flesh that he could have boasted about. Read Philippians 3:4–7 and underline the things Paul says gave him reason for confidence:

> I myself have reason for confidence in the flesh also. If anyone else thinks he has reason for confidence in the flesh, I have more: circumcised on the eighth day, of the people of Israel, of the tribe of Benjamin, a Hebrew of Hebrews; as to the law, a Pharisee; as to zeal, a persecutor of the church; as to righteousness under the law, blameless. But whatever gain I had, I counted as loss for the sake of Christ.

Now read what Paul concludes in 2 Corinthians 12:10: "For the sake of Christ, then, I am content with weaknesses, insults, hardships, persecutions, and calamities. For when I am weak, then I am strong."

What is Paul content with?

Why is he content with weakness?

The Greek word translated "weakness" means "want of strength," and here it is connected to bearing trials and troubles.[3] God calls us to humility, gentleness, patience, and love because

He knows what is best for us. He knows the desire for belonging set deeply in our souls, and He knows the path that will take us there.

Puritan minister John Flavel simplified the subject of pride with this statement: "They that know God will be humble. And they that know themselves cannot be proud."[4]

As we discuss these ideas of humility, gentleness, patience, and love, we cannot continue without remembering that we cannot produce these qualities in and of ourselves. The humility, gentleness, patience, and love we desire is a fruit of the one Spirit we share in Christ (see Gal. 5:22–23). As we learn more about this, we will continually come back to the "one Spirit … one Lord … one God and Father of all, who is over all and through all and in all" (Eph. 4:4–6). He is the head of the body, and it is only through Him that we can respond to our calling, receive our community, and hold on to the bond of peace we have in Him.

WORK IT OUT

The chart below contrasts some thoughts and actions rooted in pride with those rooted in humility. Prayerfully read through each line on this list, and ask God to point out areas of pride in your life.

PRIDE	HUMILITY
Focuses on what I have done	Focuses on what God has done for me
Pushes others away from my pain	Invites others to sympathize with and speak into my pain
Breeds alienation	Fosters unity in the body of Christ
Holds on to an offense	Forgives because I've been forgiven
Elevates self and puts others down	Lowers self in order to lift others up

What, if anything, would you add to this list?

Which item(s) on this list do you recognize most often in your life?

Since we're doing a Bible study on belonging in the body of Christ, ask God to direct you to someone you can share your answer with. Together, pray about surrendering pride for humility and moving closer to the blessings of belonging.

When we act in pride, we're willing to share only our strengths. True humility, though, frees us to share our struggles.

Day 4

Keep Doing This

Memory Verse

Make every _____ to _____

the _____ of the _____

in the _____ of _____

[each individual working together to make the whole successful].

Ephesians 4:3 AMP

I brought them home and put them in the safest place I could find. I knew the task before me would be difficult and require my full attention.

I don't have a reputation for being a green thumb. As a matter of fact, I can't think of many house plants that have survived under my care. I can, however, think of several that have not. I forget to water plants, and I certainly don't sing or talk to them. Usually in my house, plants are an afterthought. But not this time.

This time, I had purchased two poinsettia plants to give to our grandmothers as a Christmas gift. The problem was that between the day I bought the plants and the day we would deliver them, they would have to live at my house, in my care. I had to keep these plants alive for two to three *days*. Add to this already precarious situation the fact that these plants aren't what you would call "no fuss." Apparently, poinsettia plants are sensitive, delicate house plants. Even a gentle bump could cause a leaf to fall off.

Have I mentioned I have six kids? And two dogs? Never mind the fact that I barely made it from the flower shop to my car without bumping into something. The odds were against me.

Nevertheless, for the next three days, I followed the instructions from the lady who sold me the plants and did my very best to care for them. I watered them daily and diligently attempted to keep them out of harm's way. I even talked to them … every day. And on the day we delivered them to our grandmothers, they were bright, healthy, and beautiful. *Hooray!*

I wanted those plants to thrive under my care because I wanted to give our grandmothers something beautiful that would bless them and bring a smile to their faces.

We can allow that same motivation to guide our eagerness to maintain the unity of the Spirit in the bond of peace. As we consider what that eagerness looks like, I want to talk for a minute about what the opposite of eager would look like.

What are some words that might describe the opposite of eager?

You may have written words like *complacent, indifferent, reluctant, lazy,* or *idle.* Maybe you thought of words like *unconcerned* or *apathetic.* Look up the verses below, and connect them with what they say about complacency or idleness.

Hebrews 6:12	pridefully rests in excess and does not help those in need
Ezekiel 16:49	does not imitate faith and patience
Proverbs 31:27	is the opposite of being watchful

Now that we've considered what it looks like to be indifferent or unconcerned with something, let's consider how we act when we are eager about something. When I'm eager about an activity, I think about it often. I plan for it and prepare. Sometimes, when I should be thinking about something else, I'm distracted by what I'm eager about. I think about it frequently and thoroughly because it matters deeply to me.

What does it look like for you to be eager?

With these two opposing views in mind, it's time to answer the question: Am I eager to maintain the unity of the Spirit in the bond of peace?

When was the last time you acted in a way that showed your eagerness to maintain the unity of the Spirit in the bond of peace?

There are things in life that it's fine to be indifferent about, but maintaining the unity of the Spirit in the bond of peace is not one of those things.

DIGGING IN

In Ephesians 4:3 Paul urges us to be "eager to maintain the unity of the Spirit in the bond of peace."

The Greek word translated "maintain" in this verse is the same word Jesus used when He asked God to *keep* His disciples in John 17. It's not a maintenance kind of a word. Instead, it conveys the idea of fiercely guarding something you care deeply about.

The word *eager* shares that tone of urgency. Other translations use words like *diligently* maintain or *strive* to maintain the unity of the Spirit. This is not an afterthought, nor is it something we should expect to just happen. This call to eagerly maintain the bond of peace is something we should think about, practice, and intentionally pursue.

Since this is so vital to our goal of belonging, I want to give you three ways you can eagerly maintain the bond of peace.

The first is to *call out*. At times in the body of Christ, we may experience a condition I like to call the *uns*. The *uns* happen when you feel *un*welcome, *un*noticed, *un*appreciated, or *un*accepted. You could probably add a few *uns* of your own to this list as well. When we come down with a case of the *uns*, we will often self-prescribe the medicine of pulling away from the body of Christ. But to eagerly maintain the unity of the Spirit in the bond of peace, we need to change the prescription.

For an example of this new prescription, let's talk about coyotes. I know this feels like a sharp right turn, but stick with me. Where I live, I can often hear coyotes howl. As the sun beams its last light, it's not uncommon for the yips of a pack of coyotes to ring across the land near my house. I was never a huge fan of this until I learned what these yips were all about. Coyotes howl for three primary reasons: to defend and protect their territory, to communicate when hunting, and to confuse a predator.[1] One coyote researcher also noted another reason coyotes yip or howl: to promote bonding within the family group.[2]

Similar to coyotes, we need to call out to each other. When the enemy says you don't belong, call out. Share your struggles, and ask others to pray with you. When you experience victory in Jesus in a situation, call out. Tell others about what you have to celebrate and allow them to rejoice with you. Our calls to one another act as a defense against our common enemy and strengthen the common bond of peace we share in the body of Christ. To eagerly maintain the bond of peace, we must call out.

Is there something you know you need to share with another member of the body of Christ right now? Use the space below to write down the message you need to call out, along with a person or group of people you will prayerfully consider calling out to.

Next, you can *call back*. God's Word teaches us to "look not only to [our] own interests, but also to the interests of others" (Phil. 2:4). One way to do that is to be on the lookout for someone to share your experiences with and encourage with God's goodness and faithfulness. The roads you have traveled and the hardships you have walked through can help others who are going through something similar. Your encouragement may be what another member of the body of Christ needs today to give her the strength to continue.

In *Streams in the Desert*, Lettie Cowman wrote about the blessings that come from calling back to those who come behind you. Here's an excerpt:

> Life is a steep climb, and it does the heart good to have somebody "call back...." We are all climbers together, and we must help one another. This mountain climbing is serious business, but glorious. It takes strength and steady step to find the summits.... If anyone among us has found anything worth while, we ought to "call back." ...
>
> Call back, and tell me that He went with you into the storm;
> Call back, and say He kept you when the forest's roots were torn....
>
> If you have gone a little way ahead, oh, friend, call back—
> 'Twill cheer my heart and help my feet along the stony track.[3]

Maybe you are a mother of teenagers who can call back to mothers of toddlers. God may have faithfully walked you through an unexpected job change, and you can call back to someone who is going through a similar uprooting.

Pause for a moment to consider ways you can call back to others in the body of Christ. Use the space below to write circumstances that come to mind or names of people God brings to your heart.

Finally, to eagerly maintain the bond of peace in the body of Christ, you can *continually renew*. To eagerly maintain the bond of peace, we must earnestly seek the One who is peace. Read John 17:17–19:

> Sanctify them in the truth; your word is truth. As you sent me into the world, so I have sent them into the world. And for their sake I consecrate myself, that they also may be sanctified in truth.

Jesus prayed twice on His last night that His followers would be one with each other as He was one with His Father. Sandwiched between those two prayers, Jesus also prayed for their sanctification. Other translations say, "Make them holy," "Set them apart," or "Make them ready for your service."

To be sanctified is to be separated from the world, cleansed, and dedicated to God because your soul has been purified by the truth.[4] Jesus knew that the holiness of His disciples would be intricately tied to their oneness.

Paul closes Ephesians 4 with a similar call to holiness. Read verses 23–24 from the Amplified Bible:

> Be continually renewed in the spirit of your mind [having a fresh, untarnished mental and spiritual attitude], and put on the new self [the regenerated and renewed nature], created in God's image, [godlike] in the righteousness and holiness of the truth [living in a way that expresses to God your gratitude for your salvation].

We are to be continually renewed in what?

What are we to put on?

How does Paul describe the "new self"?

How great would it be if every person we bumped into today had a fresh, untarnished mental and spiritual attitude? It would solve so many problems, wouldn't it? While we can't control the mental and spiritual attitudes of others, we can eagerly maintain the bond of peace by committing to continually renew our minds. Our individual pursuit of God's righteousness and holiness impacts every other part of the body.

Belonging in the body of Christ requires us to eagerly maintain the bond of peace. To maintain the bond of peace, we must call out, call back, and be continually renewed in the spirit of our minds. As we do, we will experience God's gift of wholeness.

To eagerly maintain the bond of peace, we must call out.

WORK IT OUT

At the end of this week's study, you will find a resource titled "Call Out, Call Back." Go to that resource; then come back here and answer the following questions.

Which of the three ideas will you begin to apply today?

What is one thing you will do today to use the idea you just wrote down to call out or call back?

Day 5

Do It Together: Meet

Make every _____ to _____
the _____ of the _____ in the
_____ of _____ [each individual working
_____ to make the _____ successful].

Ephesians 4:3 AMP

I didn't really feel like going. I was tired in every way—emotionally, physically, maybe even spiritually.

Less than one week earlier, I had buried my father. When I returned home after the funeral and resumed the rhythms of ordinary life, the sting of his death remained painful. I felt a bit like I was going through the motions, so when our midweek Bible study rolled around, it felt easier to just stay home. Regardless of how I felt, though, I went. Maybe the kids really wanted to go, or maybe this was just a habit. Whatever the reason, I slipped in the door of the church, found a seat on the back row, and didn't dare say a word.

During the time when women were sharing prayer requests, the leader of my group asked how I was. I don't remember exactly what I said, but I'm pretty sure it was something like, "I'm fine." She prayed and we dismissed, but some of the women in my group weren't finished.

As I gathered my things on the back row of the room, they formed a circle around me. I guess "I'm fine" wasn't good enough for them. One woman said, "You don't have to be strong. It's okay."

I'll never forget that. These weren't women I met for coffee or lunch dates. We rarely saw each other outside of our Bible study. But these women were my sisters in Christ, fellow members of the body of Christ, and for weeks they had prayed with me about my father's health. They were part of what I was going through, and they wanted me to know they were still there.

Read Hebrews 10:23–25:

> Let us hold unswervingly to the hope we profess, for he who promised is faithful. And let us consider how we may spur one another on toward love and good deeds, not giving up meeting together, as some are in the habit of doing, but encouraging one another—and all the more as you see the Day approaching. (NIV)

Underline the words *let us* in verses 23 and 24. Circle the word that follows *let us* in each sentence.

Based on verse 24, what are we to consider?

What are we not to give up doing? Why? (v. 25)

The Greek word translated "spur" in verse 24 is used here and only one other time in Scripture. It carries the meaning to "provoke" or bring "contention."[1] The other place in Scripture you can find this word is in the verse that describes the sharp disagreement between Paul and Barnabas that we discussed last week. I love how the author of Hebrews flips the script with this word. Instead of provoking one another to anger, bitterness, or frustration, we can provoke one another to love and good works.

To do that, though, we cannot give up meeting together. It sounds simple enough, but meeting together can be more difficult than it sounds. Life happens. Routines become disrupted. We grow tired. We grow weary. We may even grow bitter and angry. And let's not forget the common enemy we share, who would love nothing more than for us to give up meeting together.

He'll do anything to convince us we don't need each other and that we can find the belonging we long for somewhere else. But this week's study has shown us there's only one place to find the belonging we seek. The world doesn't give to us like Jesus does. When we follow Him, we receive life in Him and the bond of peace in His body. It is in the body of Christ that we spur one another on to love and good works. It is in the body of Christ that we encourage each other.

One thing I don't want us to miss in this passage is the call to "all the more" (v. 25). The author of Hebrews urged his audience to meet together "all the more" as they saw the day of Jesus' return approaching. The author and his audience expected Jesus' return at the time Hebrews was written, and we should approach each day the same.

The urgency to meet together and spur one another on to love and good works only increases with each day that we draw nearer to Jesus' return. As we learned yesterday, this isn't something to take lightly. Instead, we must eagerly seek to maintain the bond of peace. To do that, we must not give up meeting together.

WORK IT OUT

Use the space below to journal about what you've learned this week. Write down what God has revealed to you. Is there an action you need to take to be obedient to God? Is there anything God has shown you through this week's study that you need to repent and turn from? Is there anything you're resisting? Ask God to bring you to a place of surrender through the power of His Spirit at work within you.

_____

Let's not forget the common enemy we share, who would love nothing more than for us to give up meeting together.

Call Out, Call Back

When we pull away from the body of Christ, it's often due to feelings of rejection or indifference from fellow Christians. When we feel like no one cares about us or notices us, it feels safer to pull away. However, when we press in and move toward the body of Christ even when feeling unnoticed or unwelcome, we can experience the blessings of belonging to Christ and His body.

Using God's Word, let's look at a few examples to help us press into the body of Christ instead of pulling away from it.

Write a letter. The New Testament is full of letters, including the one we've been studying for the last three weeks. The letters Paul wrote to the early churches were sent to encourage and build them up and also to share about his own life and needs. Maybe writing a letter with pen and paper seems outdated, but I can say—as someone who receives a handwritten letter from time to time—that it blesses those who receive it. Even if you can't get around to sending a handwritten note, you can probably find a moment to send a message from your phone to someone else's. Consider writing a note to say, "I'm thinking of you," "What are you up to?" or "How can I pray for you?"

Schedule face-to-face time. If anyone ever lived a life of high demand, it was Jesus. Yet even with so many seeking something from Him, He found time to press in with His disciples. Our lives are often so busy that games of phone tag are sure to happen. If we really want to connect with our sisters in Christ, we might need to carve out some face-to-face time. Look at the calendar. Find a few times that work for you and your friend; then schedule it on your calendar the same way you would a meeting at work or a doctor's appointment.

Pray. In his letter to the church of Ephesus, Paul wrote, "I have not stopped thanking God for you. I pray for you constantly" (Eph. 1:16 NLT). We can do the same for each other. I love my friend Lisa's idea of *prayer triggers*. As you consider praying for a sister in Christ, think of something she loves or something that reminds you of her. Every time you see or hear that thing, pray for her. Also consider taking time to meet with a small group of women and pray aloud for each other.

Week 3 Group Time

Welcome

- Leader: Introduce week 3 by asking each member to share anything she underlined or highlighted.
- Review the memory verse for the week: Ephesians 4:3.

Watch the week 3 video: "The Key to Keeping It Together."

Discussion Questions

- Practice saying the Greek word *eirḗnē* (eye-RAY-nay) in unison.
- Read the definition of *eirḗnē* from day 1. How do you define peace? How is *eirḗnē* different?
- Katy wrote, "The body of Christ is not only an essential piece of *your* belonging, but *you* are an essential part of the body of Christ." Do you believe that? If not, what keeps you from believing it?
- Read John 13:4–5. What practical steps did Jesus take in order to wash His disciples' feet? As a group, discuss your answers to the questions in the "Work It Out" section on day 2.
- Puritan minister John Flavel simplified the subject of pride with this statement: "They that know God will be humble. And they that know themselves cannot be proud." How have you experienced this?
- Review the three ways to eagerly maintain the bond of peace on day 4. Have you tried any of these? Which ones? How did it go?

Close in Prayer

- Ask for prayer requests, and thank God for your time together.
- Ask God to reveal pride in your life and help you eagerly seek to maintain the unity of the Spirit in the bond of peace.

Week 4

Living Your Most Complete Life

Memory Verse

It is love, then, that you should strive for.
Set your hearts on spiritual gifts.

1 Corinthians 14:1a GNT

Introduction

I shifted him on my hip and held tightly to his little body. I had noticed he felt small. Up until this point, though, I hadn't been alarmed.

My fifth-born son held the title of my biggest baby at birth. Weighing in at more than nine pounds, he easily beat his siblings in birth weight. He was healthy and happy, and for the first six months of his life, he grew. At our regular visits to the doctor's office, we would place him on a scale and measure him from head to toe. Each time, his growth continued. On the day we saw the doctor for his nine-month checkup, though, something had changed.

Like every other appointment, we placed him on the scale and measured him from head to toe, but the measurements this time showed no growth. Not a pound. Not an inch. In three months' time, our baby had not grown at all.

While it's not uncommon to stop growing once you reach a certain age, nine months is not that age. His growth in the previous months had created what doctors call a growth curve. So far, his growth curve had been right on track. His size and weight at this visit, however, did not follow the curve.

We were sent home with a plan for how we would jump-start his growth. We introduced new foods rich in vitamins and closely monitored how much he ate and how often. We prayed his body would absorb the nutrition and use it to grow in strength. Day after day, we repeated this routine.

Day 1

The Measure of the Fullness of Christ

Memory Verse

It is love, then, that you should strive for. Set your hearts on spiritual gifts.
1 Corinthians 14:1a GNT

After a few weeks of the new diet, we returned to the doctor's office hoping for good news. We found out the changes had, in fact, produced growth, and we rejoiced at the results. We eventually discovered too that I had become pregnant, and that ended up being the key to solving the mystery. Because my body was working to support the new life forming inside it, my nursing newborn was no longer receiving the same amount of nutrition he had before.

It's hard to ignore a lack of physical growth. The signs are usually apparent, and we rarely dismiss them. We tend to understand the importance of physical growth and the dangers associated with no growth.

The same is true in our development as a body of Christ. I'm afraid, though, we aren't always as concerned about a lack of spiritual growth in the body of Christ.

When is the last time you evaluated your own spiritual growth and the growth of the body of Christ?

So far in our study, we've dug deeply into the first six verses of Ephesians 4. This week, we will move into the next portion of Ephesians 4.

Let's read Ephesians 4:16 again:

> He makes the whole body fit together perfectly. As each part does its own special work, it helps the other parts grow, so that the whole body is healthy and growing and full of love. (NLT)

We've learned that belonging begins with brokenness, belonging brings oneness, and belonging bestows the bond of peace. Now we are ready to dive deeper into how we arrive at a body that is healthy, growing, and full of love. What we'll find is that belonging cultivates conditions that grow us from "fine" to flourishing.

Read Ephesians 4:11–14:

> He gave the apostles, the prophets, the evangelists, the shepherds and teachers, to equip the saints for the work of ministry, for building up the body of Christ, until we all attain to the unity of the faith and of the knowledge of the Son of God, to mature manhood, to the measure of the stature of the fullness of Christ, so that we may no longer be children, tossed to and fro by the waves and carried about by every wind of doctrine, by human cunning, by craftiness in deceitful schemes.

This passage lists five gifts Jesus gave to His body. What are they?

According to the passage, why did Jesus give these gifts to His church?

The passage lists three goals for the gifts given by Christ to His body, all of which follow the phrase "until we all attain." List those three things here.

Ephesians 4:7 begins Paul's discussion about gifts of the Spirit given to each follower of Christ, saying that they are to be put to good use. When we use the gifts given to us, we should do it for the purposes of attaining the unity of the faith and of the knowledge of the Son of God, mature manhood, and the measure of the stature of the fullness of Christ.

The last two weeks of our study have focused on the unity of the faith and the knowledge of the Son of God. Last week, we learned how to pursue unity in the body of Christ and why it's vital to our belonging. Some translations replace "unity of the faith" (v. 13) with *oneness* of the faith, which is what week 2 was all about. One thing I love about this statement is how it connects our oneness in faith to our knowledge of Christ. Our pursuit of oneness in the body of Christ aids our full and accurate comprehension of Christ.

Next, let's talk about mature manhood. I currently have a seventeen-year-old son in my household. I remember when he was a seven-year-old boy and the stature in which he stood was very different from what it is today. There are times now when I walk into a room and from a distance can even confuse my oldest boy with his father because his physical stature has become so closely related to his father's.

The mature manhood Paul talks about in verse 13 includes more than just physical height. One translation describes it like this: "that [we might arrive] at really mature manhood (the completeness of personality which is nothing less than the standard height of Christ's own perfection)" (AMPC). The type of maturity Paul calls us to is a spiritual maturity that exemplifies the character of Jesus.

Finally, we come to the goal of "the measure of the stature of the fullness of Christ" (v. 13). The Amplified Bible adds this descriptor, "and the completeness found in Him" (AMPC). Our spiritual growth produces completeness in Christ.

Before we go any further, I want to make one thing clear: while we study the idea of fullness and growing up into spiritual maturity, it's important to note that this is not an individual pursuit. Yes, we need to grow up individually, but the context in which Paul wrote is a corporate one. Our pursuit to attain the measure of the fullness of Christ is done together, in the body of Christ.

The Greek word used for "fullness" in verse 13 is *plērōma*, which means "that which is (has been) filled." In the book of Ephesians, Paul describes the body of believers as "that which is filled with the presence, power, agency, riches of God and of Christ."[1]

Paul talks about this fullness all the way through his letter. Look up the verses below, and connect them with what they say about fullness.

Ephesians 1:23	the fullness of God fills us when we know the love of Christ
Ephesians 3:19	the body of Christ is the fullness of Christ
Ephesians 4:10	Jesus fills all things

The root word for *plērōma* is *plēroō*, which means "to make full, to fill up, i.e. to fill to the full" or "to complete."[2] Three times in Jesus' farewell discourse, He uses this root word in connection with the fullness of His joy:

- These things I have spoken to you, that my joy may be in you, and that your joy may be full. (John 15:11)
- Until now you have asked nothing in my name. Ask, and you will receive, that your joy may be full. (John 16:24)
- Now I am coming to you, and these things I speak in the world, that they may have my joy fulfilled in themselves. (John 17:13)

Jesus fills His body with His fullness. We experience the fullness of His presence, power, riches, and joy when we participate in the body of Christ. There is something we must do before we can experience this fullness. To be full, we must first be empty of other things.

DIGGING IN

Read 1 Kings 17:14–16:

> Thus says the LORD, the God of Israel, "The jar of flour shall not be spent, and the jug of oil shall not be empty, until the day that the LORD sends rain upon the earth." And she went and did as Elijah said. And she and he and her household ate for many days. The jar of flour was not spent, neither did the jug of oil become empty, according to the word of the LORD that he spoke by Elijah.

Twice in these verses we read the words *spent* and *empty*. I'm tempted to ask you to underline these words, but who really wants to do that? *Spent* and *empty* communicate a position of lack or want. They stand in stark contrast to fullness, and they are not often things we desire or pursue. We don't want empty bank accounts or refrigerators. We don't want our emotions or the reserves in our gas tanks to be spent. Emptiness is simply not something we're inclined to seek.

The widow in 1 Kings 17 didn't seek emptiness either, yet that's the condition she found herself in. Open your Bible to that chapter and read verses 1, 8–12.

What were the conditions in the land where the widow lived?

What was she doing when she met the prophet Elijah?

What did Elijah ask her to do?

What did she expect to happen after she gathered the sticks?

This chapter tells the story of a widow who, in the wake of a devastating drought, was making preparations for her and her son's last meal. As she gathered sticks to cook her last handful of flour, she encountered Elijah. Before he delivered the word of the Lord, Elijah asked the widow to do something impossible: provide a meal for him. As the Scriptures explain, she didn't even have enough to provide for her household. Yet after Elijah told her she could trust God to provide, she did what Elijah said.

Verse 16 confirms that God kept His promise to the widow. The flour was not spent, and the jug of oil did not become empty. What the verses don't detail is the amount of flour and oil God provided. All we know is that God provided what the widow, Elijah, and her household needed at the time they needed it. The Bible doesn't imply excess or overflowing abundance. We don't read about her storing flour and oil in case the jar ever ran dry. As with manna in the wilderness, the amount of oil and flour she had was never too much or too little (see Ex. 16:4–5, 14–18).

It seems likely that each day when the widow reached for the flour and oil, she took a step of faith. She believed that what she needed would be there because God had promised He would provide it.

Our natural bent is to fill what is empty. When our lives, relationships, circumstances, or souls feel empty, we instinctively look for ways to fill them. In order for us to embrace emptiness, we have to believe God will fill us.

Only empty things can be filled. When we stay empty, we will live full.

What do you need to empty from your life today so that you can begin living in the fullness of Christ?

There's one more thing we need to address about reaching the measure of the fullness of Christ. After Paul details the goal of the body, he tells us why it's so important: "so that we may no longer be children, tossed to and fro by the waves and carried about by every wind of doctrine, by human cunning, by craftiness in deceitful schemes" (Eph. 4:14).

The Greek word translated "tossed to and fro by the waves" is used only here in Scripture, but we find the root word in two other places. James uses it to describe those who doubt (see 1:6), and Luke uses it to describe literal wind and raging waves (see 8:24). Here, in Ephesians, Paul uses it to describe those who have not grown up in their faith.

We don't have to live tossed around by the ever-changing winds and waves of life. Instead, we can grow up in our faith and in the body of Christ. As we do, we will be one step closer to a life that's not just fine but flourishing.

We experience the fullness of His presence, power, riches, and joy when we participate in the body of Christ.

WORK IT OUT

If you're still hesitant to embrace emptiness, let me encourage you with this: Jesus isn't asking you to do something He didn't already do. Jesus emptied Himself so you could be full (see Phil. 2:7).

Go back and read the verses in 1 Kings 17 and Exodus 16, and remember God's faithfulness to His people. Use the space below to write down any words or verses that stand out to you.

Consider the ways you've seen God's faithfulness to provide what you need in your own life. Then use the space below to write a prayer emptying your heart of other things so that God can fill you with His best things.

Day 2

Cultivating Your Most Complete Life

Memory Verse

It is _____, then, that you should strive for. Set your

hearts on _____ _____.

1 Corinthians 14:1a GNT

It was backbreaking work … work I wasn't entirely sure I wanted to do.

One thing I was sure of, though, was the result I desired. I'd seen the houses lined with dashes of pink and white and red and purple. I'd seen trees encircled in colorful buds and porches brought to life with baskets of blooms. I wanted that.

That, however, was not at all what I had experienced up to this point. The flower beds in front of my house looked more like piles of leaves left over from the fall. Sprinkle in a few unattended weeds, and the result was definitely not what I had seen and longed for.

But that was all about to change.

With the help of my husband, we brought a trailer full of flowers into our driveway. We spent the afternoon digging holes in the dirt, setting budding flowers gently in their places, and covering their delicate roots with soil.

One by one we arranged them, and we couldn't wait to see how they would grow.

Much to our dismay, they didn't grow how we had hoped. Don't get me wrong: they did bloom. The end result was "fine." But instead of thriving flowers welcoming us home each day, these blooms looked like they were barely hanging on.

They bloomed, but they didn't flourish.

I've already mentioned that I'm not a green thumb. I do, however, know someone who is. After years of trying to get beautiful flowers to grow in my yard, we heard about a man with an impressive track record.

We saw the yards he'd worked on that displayed blooms of all kinds. The flowers circled trees and lined up in perfect rows across the front porch. He clearly knew what he was doing.

We contacted him, and he came to look at our yard. In that consultation, he told us there was something we needed to do before he would plant the beautiful blooms we longed for. He saw that our biggest problem in growing plants was not our care for the plants once they were planted, but the soil we planted them in. We weren't starting with good soil—or even with the same quality of soil on either side of the gate. So no matter how hard we worked to grow healthy, thriving flowers, we would be hard pressed to get the best results. Good soil is the difference between fine and flourishing.

Read Ephesians 4:13, this time from the Amplified Bible:

> Until we all reach oneness in the faith and in the knowledge of the Son of God, [growing spiritually] to become a mature believer, reaching to the measure of the fullness of Christ [manifesting His spiritual completeness and exercising our spiritual gifts in unity].

There are some familiar words in this version of Ephesians 4:13. Underline the words *oneness, growing, fullness,* and *completeness.*

In week 2 of our study, we discussed how belonging brings oneness. Last week, we learned about the bond of peace that produces a completeness unlike anything the world has to offer. Yesterday, we talked about fullness.

Let's review our goal for this week and this study. Read Ephesians 4:16:

> He makes the whole body fit together perfectly. As each part does its own special work, it helps the other parts grow, so that the whole body is healthy and growing and full of love. (NLT)

Today, let's get our hands dirty and dig into the soil that produces growth.

Read 2 Peter 1:5–8:

> For this very reason, make every effort to supplement your faith with virtue, and virtue with knowledge, and knowledge with self-control, and self-control with steadfastness, and steadfastness with godliness, and godliness with brotherly affection, and brotherly affection with love. For if these qualities are yours and are increasing, they keep you from being ineffective or unfruitful in the knowledge of our Lord Jesus Christ.

What seven qualities does Peter say should be yours and should be increasing?

If these qualities are yours and are increasing, what does the Bible say they will keep you from being?

These qualities—virtue, knowledge, self-control, steadfastness, godliness, brotherly affection, and love—are blooms of spiritual maturity. As the New Living Translation words verse 8, "The more you grow like this, the more productive and useful you will be in your knowledge of our Lord Jesus Christ." I love that, just like the humility, gentleness, patience, and love we learned about last week, these blooms of spiritual maturity require relationship with one another.

As with the growth of any plant, spiritual growth begins in the soil. To grow in maturity and reach the measure of the fullness of Christ, we need to address the soil in which we are planting.

DIGGING IN

Read Mark 4:3–8:

> Listen! Behold, a sower went out to sow. And as he sowed, some seed fell along the path, and the birds came and devoured it. Other seed fell on rocky ground, where it did not have much soil, and immediately it sprang up, since it had no depth of soil. And when the sun rose, it was scorched, and since it had no root, it withered away. Other seed fell among thorns, and the thorns grew up and choked it, and it yielded no grain. And other seeds fell into good soil and produced grain, growing up and increasing and yielding thirtyfold and sixtyfold and a hundredfold.

In what four places did the seed fall?

In the verses above, Jesus told the crowd about a sower who went out to sow seed. This context would have been very familiar to Jesus' original audience since they were an agrarian community. Jesus mentions four places where the seed fell: along the path, on rocky ground, among thorns, and into good soil. Each place where the seed fell yielded a different result.

Use the chart below to record the result of where each seed fell.

PLACE	RESULT
Path	
Rocky ground	
Thorns	
Good soil	

Only the seeds that fell into good soil produced, grew, and increased. The seeds that fell in the other places encountered problems that kept them from growing. In verses 14–20,

Jesus explains the meaning of this parable to His disciples. His explanation sheds light on the problems associated with where the seeds fell. Open your Bible, and read Mark 4:14–20; then come back here.

Jesus calls attention to three opponents of good soil in our hearts: Satan, trials, and the cares of the world.

Some of the seed fell on the road. That represents those whose hearts are still too hard to receive the good news. Satan works swiftly to remove it from their minds.

Yesterday, we talked about "other things" that fill our hearts and hinder us from being filled to the measure of the fullness of Christ. Jesus draws out some of those "other things," specifically concerning the seeds that fell on rocky ground and the ones that fell among thorns. Based on what you just read, fill in the chart below with the "other things" associated with the rocky ground and thorns.

PLACE	OTHER THINGS
Rocky ground (v. 17)	
Thorns (v. 19)	

The seeds that fell on rocky ground had no root. Consequently, their growth was short-lived. For a time, they may have seemed fine, but they never flourished, and they fell away quickly. As an infant in Christ, a person with this kind of heart-soil is like a young plant whose roots don't go very deep. That person's faith journey may begin with joy, but when trouble or distress arises or when they begin to suffer for their faith, they give up.

The seeds that fell among thorns encountered a different problem. Jesus detailed three types of thorns: cares of the world, deceitfulness of riches, and desires for other things. There it is again: *other things*. In *The Message*, Eugene Peterson describes people with hearts in this condition as those who "are overwhelmed with worries about all the things they have to do and all the things they want to get. The stress strangles what they heard, and nothing comes of it" (v. 19).

I think these thorns, like pride, can be sneaky. If I asked you to make a list of all the things you have to do and all the things you want to get, it probably wouldn't require much thought. Oftentimes, these are the things that stay on our minds.

This reminds me of the *me* mindset we talked about last week. We can be sure that a *me* mindset will not produce spiritual growth.

Which one of the conditions above do you struggle with most?

How have you seen these conditions interfere with your spiritual growth, as well as the growth of the whole body of Christ?

Now let's contrast these with the soil we read about in verse 20: "Those that were sown on the good soil are the ones who hear the word and accept it and bear fruit, thirtyfold and sixtyfold and a hundredfold."

In what three ways does Jesus describe "those that were sown on the good soil"?

The seeds sown on the good soil flourished. They produced as much as one hundred times more than what was sown. In his gospel, Luke expands on the idea of accepting the Word of God. He writes, "As for that in the good soil, they are those who, hearing the word, hold it fast in an honest and good heart, and bear fruit with patience" (8:15). The word Luke chose for how we respond to the Word carries the idea of not just accepting it but also possessing it.[1]

According to this verse, the good soil represents those who hear the Word and do what with it?

In what kind of heart do they hold it fast?

How do we bear fruit?

The Bible has plenty to say about holding fast. Look up the Scriptures below, and connect them to how they instruct us to hold fast.

1 Corinthians 15:2	the word
1 Thessalonians 5:21	our confidence
Hebrews 10:23	what is good
Hebrews 3:6	the confession of our hope

Let's consider how a heart that holds fast to God's Word approaches times of trial and worries of this world. Read James 1:2–4: "Consider it pure joy, my brothers and sisters, whenever you face trials of many kinds, because you know that the testing of your faith produces perseverance. Let perseverance finish its work so that you may be mature and complete, not lacking anything" (NIV).

While a heart with rocky ground produces a short-lived harvest that withers in the heat of life's trials, a heart full of good soil considers it pure joy. This heart anticipates what the trial will bring—a life that is complete, lacking nothing.

To see how a heart that holds fast to the Word handles the worries of this world, read Philippians 4:6–7: "Don't worry about anything, but in everything, through prayer and petition with thanksgiving, present your requests to God. And the peace of God, which surpasses all understanding, will guard your hearts and minds in Christ Jesus" (CSB).

The peace of God that this verse talks about is the same peace we learned about last week—peace given to us as God's gift of wholeness.

Let's not settle for life that's simply fine. To grow to the measure of the fullness of Christ, we need to foster conditions—both in our own hearts individually and in the body of Christ—that allow the Word of God to flourish.

WORK IT OUT

Growth begins in the soil, and we must continually tend to the conditions for growth in our individual hearts. To move from fine to flourishing, we must also grow up together in the body of Christ.

The chart below details some specific ways the body of Christ nourishes our growth. Look up the Scriptures; then answer the question "How does this help us grow?" from each verse.

IN THE BODY OF CHRIST WE ...	SCRIPTURE	HOW DOES THIS HELP US GROW?
Confess our sins to one another	James 5:16	
Encourage each other when we grow weary	Galatians 6:9	
Learn from one another	Colossians 3:16	
Invite the work of the Holy Spirit	Matthew 18:20	
Help each other when we fall	Ecclesiastes 4:10	

Your answers may not come immediately, and that's okay. It may require more time in prayer as you ask God to show you how belonging in the body of Christ causes you to flourish. Read the verses slowly, and read them several times.

Which of these things are you doing well?

Which ones do you need to do more of?

What steps can you take toward spiritual growth in the body of Christ?

Day 3

Let Us Use Them

Memory Verse

It is _____, then, that you should
_____ _____. Set your hearts on
_____ _____.

1 Corinthians 14:1a GNT

They huddled together just outside the dugout, eagerly awaiting their assignments.

My son's baseball team prepared to take the field. But before they could, they needed to know the positions assigned to them. The coach held up his clipboard and began announcing who went where. He sent one player to the pitcher's mound and another to first base. One boy he told to take his place behind home plate, and another he told to hustle to center field. One by one, the eager players were sent to their unique positions on the field. The coach's placement of them was intentional and well planned.

The coach knew his players' strengths and where they would fit best. His goal, along with the goal of every boy on the field that day, was to win the game. In order to do that, each player needed to be in the position best suited for him.

Through the course of our time together, we've talked about what we have in common. We've learned about the common identity, common enemy, and common bond we share. Today, we will see that all these things lead us to a *common good*.

Read 1 Corinthians 12:4–7:

> There are varieties of gifts, but the same Spirit; and there are varieties of ser-
> vice, but the same Lord; and there are varieties of activities, but it is the same
> God who empowers them all in everyone. To each is given the manifestation
> of the Spirit for the common good.

The focus of our study has been Ephesians, but the passage above falls within another letter Paul wrote, this one to the church in Corinth. Here, as in his letter to the Ephesians, Paul discusses the gifts given by Christ to the church for the equipping and building up of the body. Like the baseball players on the field that day, in the body of Christ we are all on the same team. Just as the players on the baseball team shared a common goal and used their talents to benefit the whole team, we aim for a common good in the body of Christ.

The term "common good" comes from a Greek word that means "to bear together or at the same time." It carries the idea of *benefit* or *help*, and in this context, it's related to that which is "profitable."[1]

We each have gifts given to us by God to accomplish His purposes in His church and in the world. These gifts are often called spiritual gifts, and as we'll see today, our use of these spiritual gifts is important to our goal of spiritual maturity and the common good of the body of Christ.

DIGGING IN

Read Ephesians 4:11–14:

> He gave the apostles, the prophets, the evangelists, the shepherds and teach-
> ers, to equip the saints for the work of ministry, for building up the body of
> Christ, until we all attain to the unity of the faith and of the knowledge of
> the Son of God, to mature manhood, to the measure of the stature of the
> fullness of Christ, so that we may no longer be children, tossed to and fro by
> the waves and carried about by every wind of doctrine, by human cunning,
> by craftiness in deceitful schemes.

Underline the gifts Paul says Jesus gave to His body.

Just before these verses in Ephesians 4, Paul confirms that the apostles, prophets, evangelists, shepherds, and teachers have received their spiritual gifts from Christ by the measure of His grace (see v. 7). On day 1 of this week, you listed the purposes of these gifts—to equip the saints for the work of ministry and for building up the body of Christ.

Another New Testament writer, Peter, gives one more purpose for these spiritual gifts. Read 1 Peter 4:10–11:

> As each has received a gift, use it to serve one another, as good stewards of God's varied grace: whoever speaks, as one who speaks oracles of God; whoever serves, as one who serves by the strength that God supplies—in order that in everything God may be glorified through Jesus Christ. To him belong glory and dominion forever and ever. Amen.

What reason does Peter give for the use of spiritual gifts? (Hint: It follows the phrase "in order that.")

In Romans 12 and 1 Corinthians 12, Paul lists additional spiritual gifts given to the body of Christ by the grace of Christ. The outline below details eighteen spiritual gifts mentioned in the New Testament and where they're found.[2]

- Apostleship: 1 Corinthians 12:28; Ephesians 4:11
- Tongues: 1 Corinthians 12:10, 28, 30
- Interpretation: 1 Corinthians 12:10, 30
- Miracles: 1 Corinthians 12:10, 28
- Healing: 1 Corinthians 12:9, 28
- Faith: 1 Corinthians 12:9
- Discernment: 1 Corinthians 12:10

- Word of Wisdom: 1 Corinthians 12:8
- Word of Knowledge: 1 Corinthians 12:8
- Evangelism: Ephesians 4:11
- Prophecy: Romans 12:6; Ephesians 4:11; 1 Corinthians 12:10, 28
- Teaching: Romans 12:7; 1 Corinthians 12:28
- Exhortation: Romans 12:8
- Shepherding: Ephesians 4:11
- Serving: Romans 12:7; 1 Corinthians 12:28
- Mercy-showing: Romans 12:8
- Giving: Romans 12:8
- Administration: Romans 12:8; 1 Corinthians 12:28

Many scholars agree on this list of eighteen spiritual gifts recorded in Scripture. However, others find up to twenty-seven spiritual gifts listed in the pages of God's Word. I want you to have the list above just to get you started, but no matter how many spiritual gifts are found in Scripture, nearly all scholars conclude that this is not an exhaustive list.[3] There are many helpful resources and spiritual gift assessments available to help you determine your spiritual gifts. Let's take a look at some things to consider as we study our spiritual gifting.

Spiritual gifts are for everyone, not a select few. You may have believed that spiritual gifts are reserved for leaders in the church or people who go to seminary, but that couldn't be further from the truth. Spiritual gifts are given to all who share the one Spirit that Paul wrote about in Ephesians 4:4. If you have received Jesus as your Savior, you have been given the Spirit—and with Him comes spiritual gifts. This means every single follower of Jesus has been given a gift of the Spirit and has a responsibility to use that gift so that the body of Christ is healthy and growing.

Spiritual gifts are things we cannot do apart from the Holy Spirit. Since we just established that gifts of the Spirit are given by the Spirit, we must then acknowledge that spiritual gifts are not the same as talents or abilities. Gifts of the Spirit require the work of the Spirit. They are an example of the Holy Spirit working in us and through us. They are not something we can produce on our own. This would make them different from a skill you learned in school or a natural ability that has always come easily for you. Here is how one popular website distinguishes between talents and spiritual gifts:

1. A talent is the result of genetics and/or training, while a spiritual gift is the result of the power of the Holy Spirit.

2. A talent can be possessed by anyone, Christian or non-Christian, while spiritual gifts are only possessed by Christians.

3. While both talents and spiritual gifts should be used for God's glory and to minister to others, spiritual gifts are focused on these tasks, while talents can be used entirely for non-spiritual purposes.[4]

To employ the gifts of the Spirit, we must walk in step with the Spirit.

Spiritual gifts demonstrate the diversity of the members of the body of Christ. We don't all have the same spiritual gifts. This, sister, is why it's so vital that we use them. The gifting of the Holy Spirit in you is not the same as the gifting in me. Romans 12:6 records four very important words. Just before Paul discusses gifts given to the church, He says, "let us use them." The whole body of Christ needs *you* to use the gifts given to *you*. We are whole when each one of us uses the gifts given to us by God to accomplish the purposes of God.

At this point, I suspect you are either fairly certain about at least one gift you have been given by the Spirit or you have absolutely no idea. If you have no idea what your spiritual gift might be, here are a few places to begin:

1. Go back to the list of spiritual gifts found in Scripture, and read it slowly. Circle any gifts that make you excited or that you think might be something you've seen in your life.

2. Ask other believers if they have seen any of these spiritual gifts in you and the context in which they noticed them.

3. Pray and ask God to show you what gift He's given you.

4. Go for it! Even if you aren't sure if you have a specific spiritual gift, if an opportunity arises for you to try something that would use that gift, do it. Maybe you'll discover it's not your spiritual gifting, after all, but you will be one step closer to finding out what is.

As we close today's study, I want to bring us back to the mission of the church. Using our spiritual gifts helps the body grow and build itself up in love, but that's not all it does. Let's recall some of Jesus' last words:

> As you sent me into the world, so I have sent them into the world … so that the world may believe that you have sent me … so that the world may know that you sent me and loved them even as you loved me. (John 17:18, 21, 23)

As we use our gifts to build up the body of Christ in love, we are a witness to those who don't know Jesus. When we love and serve each other, we show the unbelieving world the love of Christ.

WORK IT OUT

When Paul discusses the body of Christ, he speaks about it in two contexts—the universal church and the local church. The universal church describes the body of believers made up of every Christian in every part of the world. No matter where you live, you are connected to believers in other countries, cultures, and continents because of Jesus.

The local church, however, is the body of Christ in a specific place. For most of us, the local church looks like a group of believers from the same city or area that regularly gather in a designated place.

Our spiritual gifts are most practically used, and their purposes most intimately realized, in the context of the local church.

In the last two decades, I've attended at least ten local churches in five states. My husband's job moved us often and suddenly, and many times I would visit a new church in a new city with my six children all by myself. I've attended gatherings of local churches that met in a tent, a nightclub, a school, and a traditional church building, just to name a few.

It wasn't always fun, and it wasn't always easy. I remember times of sitting on the back row (and by back row, I mean the very back row in the balcony), alone, with tears running down my cheeks. I recall pulling up to church with rain pouring down while I ran for the door, holding my children. I've shown up for church with one of my children missing shoes, and I've shown up for church at the wrong time. I've shown up eager and expectant, and I've shown up tired and weary.

God had impressed on my heart how important being a part of a local body of Christ would be for my family and me. So no matter how tired I was or how new the city was, the kids and I would pile into the car on Sunday morning and go to church.

If you aren't currently a member of a local body of believers, I encourage you to begin the process of plugging into one. For help with this, go to the resource titled "Finding Your Place" at the end of this week's study. Then come back here.

Who will you ask this week about where they attend church?

Look at your calendar, and choose a day to visit a local church. If you have a paper calendar, circle the day you will go. If you're using a digital calendar, make an appointment and title it "Connect to Local Church." I encourage you to pick a date within the next two weeks.

Use the space below to write a prayer. If you already attend a local church, ask God to show you one new way you can use your spiritual gift to build up your local body and glorify Him. Also ask God to show you one person you can invite to join you at your local church.

If you're not a member of a local church, ask God to give you a heart that desires to gather regularly with other members of the body of Christ, and ask Him to reveal anything that's hindering you from gathering with His body.

We are whole when each one of us uses the gifts given to us by God to accomplish the purposes of God.

Day 4

What Are You Striving For?

Memory Verse

It is _____, then, that

you should _____ _____.

Set your _____ on

_____ _____."

1 Corinthians 14:1a GNT

Falling! I yelled.

Fall on! they responded.

I stood perched atop a picnic table beneath the limbs of a nearby tree. I had come to this adventure park with a group I belonged to for a day of what they called team-building exercises. The goal of this day was for the team to grow in trust and dependence on each other. The means to the goal was what I found myself about to do: a trust fall.

From on top of the picnic table, the trust fall required me to fall backward, like a log, into the (hopefully) waiting arms of my teammates. They were, in theory, supposed to catch me. We had been instructed on the proper technique for each part of this exercise. Experts had taught me the right way to fall so the landing would be easy for my teammates. The instructor had taught my teammates how to absorb my fall so I would land painlessly in their arms and not on the ground.

We had learned what we were supposed to learn and said what we were supposed to say; the only thing left to do was fall.

It would have been easier to trust them to catch me if they hadn't been giggling and talking among themselves. From the top of that table, the risk felt like it was all mine. The people who were supposed to soften my fall didn't seem to be taking this seriously. Their attitudes made my trust fall more difficult.

In our goal of spiritual maturity and a body that is healthy, growing, and built up in love, we need to address one more very important thing.

Read Ephesians 4:15–16:

> Speaking the truth in love, we are to grow up in every way into him who is
> the head, into Christ, from whom the whole body, joined and held together
> by every joint with which it is equipped, when each part is working properly,
> makes the body grow so that it builds itself up in love.

These verses are bookended with a two-word phrase that begins with the word *in*. What is that phrase?

What two things are we, the body of Christ, to do "in love"?

Sometimes, I think growing together in the body of Christ can feel like my trust fall that day. We learn what we're supposed to do and the right ways to do it, but trusting one another can feel risky, if not irresponsible.

The two things Paul reminds us to do in love—speaking the truth and building the body up—can't really be done apart from love. When we doubt someone's love for us or question whether their intentions are loving and kind, we are far less likely to believe that what they say to us is true. When love is absent, things are more likely to be torn down than built up.

Read verse 29: "Let no corrupting talk come out of your mouths, but only such as is good for building up, as fits the occasion, that it may give grace to those who hear."

According to this verse, what is the opposite of what is good for building up?

What should be the goal of what comes out of our mouths?

The original word used for "corrupting" can also mean "rotten," "worthless," or "unfit for use."[1] Look up the verses below and record how they expand on corrupting talk.

Ephesians 5:4 ──────▶

Colossians 3:8 ──────▶

Before we go any further, let's recall what Jesus did for us *in love*:

> Blessed and worthy of praise be the God and Father of our Lord Jesus Christ, who has blessed us with every spiritual blessing in the heavenly realms in Christ, just as [in His love] He chose us in Christ [actually selected us for Himself as His own] before the foundation of the world, so that we would be

holy [that is, consecrated, set apart for Him, purpose-driven] and blameless in His sight. In love He predestined and lovingly planned for us to be adopted to Himself as [His own] children through Jesus Christ, in accordance with the kind intention and good pleasure of His will—to the praise of His glorious grace and favor, which He so freely bestowed on us in the Beloved [His Son, Jesus Christ]. (Eph. 1:3–6 AMP)

Why did Jesus choose us and plan for us to be adopted to Himself? (Hint: See the phrase that follows *so that*.)

What did Jesus do in love? (Hint: It starts with the phrase "In love He ...")

Our words can strengthen the spiritual progress of the body of Christ, or they can stunt the growth of others—or even worse, tear them down completely. We can use our words to fight for ourselves, our agenda, and our opinions, or we can let Jesus' example of love move us to strive for something different.

DIGGING IN

Read 2 Timothy 2:14: "Remind them of these things, charging them before the Lord not to strive about words to no profit, to the ruin of the hearers" (NKJV).

Now compare this verse to what you read in Philippians 1:27: "Only let your manner of life be worthy of the gospel of Christ, so that whether I come and see you or am absent, I may hear of you that you are standing firm in one spirit, with one mind striving side by side for the faith of the gospel."

What does 2 Timothy 2:14 tell us *not* to strive about?

What does Philippians 1:27 tell us *to* strive for?

The Greek word translated "strive about words" in 2 Timothy 2:14 is used only this one time in all of Scripture. It appears like a compound word, combining two Greek words that are translated "words" and "strive," and it means "to contend about words."[2] Depending on what translation you read, this term can be rendered a variety of ways, including:

- "quarrel about words" (ESV)
- "fight about words" (CSB)
- "engage in battles over words" (CEB)
- "wrangle about words" (NASB1995)

These are some strong ideas about the words that come out of our mouths. This description is exhausting to think about.

Describe a time that you were either part of or witness to a situation that involved engaging in battles about words.

The idea of battling with our words creates mental, emotional, and spiritual fatigue. I know because I'm all too familiar with striving about words. As a teenager and even into my young adult years, I was willing to offer my opinion on just about anything, and I refused to lose. While I never actually participated in the debate team at school, people told me I should because I could win any war of words.

My sister eventually gave up arguing with me because she knew I would never quit. I would force my opinion into any situation and voice it until everyone else agreed with me. While the world saw my "spirited" and aggressive assertions as something to be praised, God's Word says something very different.

Look up the following verses in the book of Proverbs, and connect them with what they say about our words.

Proverbs 26:21	we can share godly wisdom and kind instruction
Proverbs 26:22	gracious words are sweet to the mind and healing to the body
Proverbs 26:28	gossip penetrates deep within you
Proverbs 16:24	quarrelsome words kindle strife
Proverbs 31:26	lying words work ruin

In a world that tells us our opinions should be voiced on all matters all the time, we as believers have to decide if we are willing to sacrifice being right with our Master in order to be right on the matter. Is there a time to admonish one another with God's Word? Yes (see Col. 3:16). Does God want us to strongly urge one another to follow Him? Absolutely (see Heb. 3:13). But is any of that about *me* being right and *my* opinion being heard? Not even a little bit.

Our words leave a lasting impact. They can divide, destroy, and deceive, or they can bring delight and give grace to those who hear them. Words that give grace are words that produce growth.

Read Colossians 3:15–16:

> Let the peace of Christ rule in your hearts, to which indeed you were called in one body. And be thankful. Let the word of Christ dwell in you richly, teaching and admonishing one another in all wisdom, singing psalms and hymns and spiritual songs, with thankfulness in your hearts to God.

What were we called to in one body?

What two phrases follow the words *let the*?

What are the results of letting the word of Christ dwell in you richly?

I eventually did the trust fall that day … and my teammates did catch me. The trust fall Jesus invites us into is so much safer than my fall from the table because this fall isn't into the arms of others. When we fall, we fall into the arms of Jesus.

God has changed that girl who once welcomed every opportunity to strive about words. I've seen the difference between His words and mine and experienced how much better it is to let the peace of Christ rule in my heart and let the Word of Christ dwell within me.

Even if this still feels dangerous, I encourage you to remember the love of Christ and trust Him enough to surrender your words to Him. Let Him use your words to share His love, build others up, and help the body of Christ grow.

We as believers have to decide if we are willing to sacrifice being right with our Master in order to be right on the matter.

WORK IT OUT

Research reports that, on average, we speak approximately sixteen thousand words a day.[3] That's *one day* of words. In today's world, our words aren't always spoken, though. Sometimes, our words are typed in a text message or a social media post. With the amount of words we produce each day, it is crucial that we prioritize this matter of speaking the truth in love. The building up of the body of Christ depends on it. So before we speak ... or type, or post ... let's commit to ask ourselves these two questions:

- Am I striving to be right and win a war of words? or
- Am I striving to be right with God and yield to His Word?

You might write these questions down and keep them in a place you will see often. You might even take a picture of them and make that photo the lock screen image on your phone. Review them often. Remember them regularly, and as you do, enjoy the belonging that grows out of words spoken in love.

Day 5

Do It Together: Rejoice!

Memory Verse

It is _____, then, that you should _____

_____. _____ _____ _____

on _____ _____.

1 Corinthians 14:1a GNT

I paused for a minute to take in the scene unfolding around me. I hadn't expected this.

Several months earlier, Luke and I found out we were expecting our fourth child. While this was our fourth baby, it was our first baby girl. We had lived in the city where he was playing for only one year, and our daughter's due date fell in the middle of football season. Time was short and demands were high, so I never expected some of the other players' wives to organize a baby shower.

Not only did they organize a baby shower to celebrate the birth of our baby girl, but they also reached out to dear friends of mine who lived in the city we'd left the year before, and those friends came too! They piled into our rental house, which was way too small for all of us, and attended the baby shower full of all things pink and pastel.

I really couldn't believe it. I wasn't used to this kind of pause. I usually moved through life going from one task to the next, taking care of business, trying not to get behind. But here, in this moment, my friends and sisters in Christ had created space for rejoicing.

Read 2 Corinthians 13:11: "Finally, brothers and sisters, rejoice. Become mature, be encouraged, be of the same mind, be at peace, and the God of love and peace will be with you" (CSB).

On our journey to belonging, we can rejoice. Perhaps you may have come this far in our study together and are completely committed to the goal of belonging. Your heart may be open to considering and applying each piece required for belonging in Christ and in His body. You may not, however, feel you have time for rejoicing.

For some, rejoicing isn't part of the regular rhythm of life. There may be too many boxes to check, or you may feel like there is too much work to be done. You may still be sitting in the shattered pieces of sin or tragic circumstances, and while you can wrap your mind around the pursuit of belonging, rejoicing might be something you'd rather not include at the moment.

Throughout the New Testament, God's Word tells us what we have to rejoice about and when we should rejoice. We can:

- rejoice in hope (Rom. 12:12)
- rejoice in sufferings (1 Pet. 4:13)
- rejoice when the glory of Christ is revealed (1 Pet. 4:13)
- rejoice in the Lord (Phil. 4:4)
- rejoice always (1 Thess. 5:16)

God's Word doesn't tell us to wait for a specific set of circumstances or pace of life before we are to rejoice. Instead, we're taught to rejoice always because of the hope we have in Jesus.

Let's go to the last book of the Bible and see what we will be doing together as we pass from this life into eternity with Christ. Read Revelation 19:7: "Let us be glad, rejoice, and give him glory, because the marriage of the Lamb has come, and his bride has prepared herself" (CSB).

I'm smiling as I write this. I don't know where you are right now, spiritually or emotionally. I don't know the details of your life. But I do know that on a day that is coming soon, I will be rejoicing with you, together with all the saints in the presence of our Savior.

Since we will rejoice together forever in eternity, I say we go ahead and start the celebration now. (If you have a happy dance, now's the time, girl!)

WORK IT OUT

I hope this week has been as much fun for you as it has been for me. The thought of you and me putting our spiritual gifts to use in the body of Christ and growing together—healthy, strong, and full of love—feels so very exciting. It's an edge-of-your-seat kind of feeling, and I hope you feel it too, but let's not settle for a feeling. Let's make a plan for what we will do with what we've learned this week.

Ask God to help you determine three steps that you will take in the days and weeks to come to find out more about your spiritual gifts and use them in your local body of Christ. Your first step may be finding a church to join. If you're already a part of a local church and aware of your spiritual gifts, your first step may be praying about how you will use those gifts to benefit the whole body.

Use the space below to write down the three steps you will take toward the common good of the body of Christ, as well as the practical ways you will accomplish each step.

Finding Your Place

Ask. Decide. Go. Consider. Go back. Repeat.

Step 1: If you don't yet belong to a local church, ask someone you work with, a parent at your child's school, or a neighbor, "Where do you go to church?" If you don't know anyone to ask, you can use the internet or drive around and look for churches in your area.

Step 2: Decide what church you will visit. Find out where it is and what time services start, and make a plan to visit.

Step 3: Go. Don't expect it to be easy, but determine ahead of time that whether it's raining or you're running late, you will go.

Step 4: As you visit local churches, consider these spiritual and practical matters:

Spiritual
- Does this church preach the Bible?
- Does this church have a statement of faith that agrees with what the Bible says?
- Does this church seek and serve those who are lost?
- Is this church eager to maintain the unity of the Spirit in the bond of peace?
- Do you feel God leading you to this local body of Christ?
- Can you serve in this local body of Christ?

Practical
- Is the location one that you will consistently go to?

- Do you feel comfortable navigating the building and the parking lot regularly?
- Are your children or other family members comfortable when you are there?

Step 5: Go back. I've found it usually takes more than one visit to truly determine if a local church is right for me. I recommend you visit the same church for at least two to four weeks when possible.

Step 6: Repeat steps 1 through 5 until you find your place in a local church.

Week 4 Group Time

Welcome

- Leader: Introduce week 4 by asking each member to share anything she underlined or highlighted.
- Review the memory verse for the week: 1 Corinthians 14:1a.

Watch the week 4 video: "Living Your Most Complete Life."

Discussion Questions

- Would you say your life is fine or flourishing? Why?
- Katy wrote, "Only empty things can be filled. When we stay empty, we will live full." What do you need to empty from your life so that you can begin living in the fullness of Christ?
- Read Mark 4:14–20. Which opponent of good soil do you struggle with the most? How have you seen these conditions interfere with your spiritual growth?
- Look up and read the verses listed in the chart in the "Work It Out" section of day 2. How do these things help us flourish together in the body of Christ?
- Review the list of eighteen spiritual gifts on day 3, and discuss the three things to consider as we study our spiritual gifting.
- Read 2 Timothy 2:14 and Philippians 1:27. Discuss what is means to strive about words and how that impacts growth in the body of Christ.

Close in Prayer

- Ask for prayer requests, and thank God for your time together.
- Ask God to show you how to take steps toward the common good of the body of Christ.

Week 5

What Happens When We Belong

Memory Verse

I am sure of this, that he who started a good work in you will carry it on to completion until the day of Christ Jesus.

Philippians 1:6 CSB

Introduction

The buzzing from my husband's cell phone made my heart beat faster. Who would be calling him at this hour?

Minutes before, we had celebrated my husband making an NFL team and the beginning of another season and another adventure together. After dinner, we prayed with our little boys, gave them one last kiss, and tucked them snugly into bed. I had just returned to a sink full of dishes when the phone buzzed.

On a side note, I learned the hard way that you need to rinse spaghetti dishes before you load them into the dishwasher. Otherwise, everything in the dishwasher will turn a shade of orange. Armed with this hard-earned knowledge, I had every intention of pre-rinsing the spaghetti dishes piled in the sink, but the missed call on Luke's cell phone diverted my attention.

When he returned to the kitchen, my shaky voice alerted Luke to the buzz I had heard. The look on my face reflected my concern. He retrieved the phone and walked out the back door. I watched through the window as he returned the call. His head was down, and he nodded as he listened. When he walked back into the house, Luke revealed exactly what I had been afraid of all along.

The phone call brought word that Luke had been traded. In football terms, this meant his contract had been transferred to another team and he would now be a player on that new team's roster. In life terms, that meant we were moving … to a new city … immediately. And by "immediately," I mean the next morning.

My plans for the night instantly changed.

The dining room table became the staging point for stacks of clothes that would soon be at least slightly organized and packed into suitcases. I didn't know how long we'd be gone.

I didn't even know exactly where we were going. I just knew we needed to put some things in a bag. I counted out diapers and Pull-Ups, underwear, and bottles and sippy cups. We needed shoes and swimsuits, shorts and T-shirts, and on and on the list went. I sorted and counted until my eyes turned blurry; then I laid my head on the pillow and tried to sleep for a few hours.

The next morning, we drove several hours to the new city we would call home, and I unloaded what had just been packed the night before. We spent the next two weeks in a hotel room, where I tried to put the pieces of our lives back into some kind of order. We needed to find a place to live, a grocery store, a preschool, and a church. We had new friends to meet, new roads to discover, and new plans to make. On the outside, I treated it like an adventure, but on the inside, I didn't know where to begin.

Day 1

Ready for a New Start

Memory Verse

I am sure of this, that he who started a good work in you will carry it on to completion until the day of Christ Jesus.

Philippians 1:6 CSB

For the last four weeks, we've walked the path to belonging together. Along the way, we've discovered several things we have in common. We share a common brokenness, a common identity in Christ, a common enemy, a common bond, and a common good.

This week, we will walk step by step with the nation of Israel and witness what happens when we belong to Jesus and His body. As we journey back to the Old Testament and peek in again on God's people, we will meet Israel at the place of a new beginning.

Before we do, let's review what we learned in week 1 of our study.

Read Ephesians 4:1: "I therefore, a prisoner for the Lord, urge you to walk in a manner worthy of the calling to which you have been called." Week 1 taught us that to belong, we must respond to our calling. We learned two vital pieces to this response. First, to respond to our calling, we need to put on our identity in Christ and participate in the body of Christ. Second, we learned that the body of Christ is directed by the head of the body, Jesus, and that to walk in a manner worthy of our calling, we must pursue our head.

As we begin our walk with the nation of Israel, we meet them at a time in their history when they had been exiled from their land. They had turned away from pursuing and serving

God and had suffered the consequences of their disobedience. Their enemies overtook them, destroyed their cities, and led them out of their homeland as captives.

Today, as we pick up their story, some of the exiles have returned to the land given to them by God. Upon their arrival, they found a land still in piles of rubble and ruin. They needed a place to begin rebuilding. Let's find out what happened.

DIGGING IN

Read Ezra 3:8:

> In the second year after their coming to the house of God at Jerusalem, in the second month, Zerubbabel the son of Shealtiel and Jeshua the son of Jozadak made a beginning, together with the rest of their kinsmen, the priests and the Levites and all who had come to Jerusalem from the captivity. They appointed the Levites, from twenty years old and upward, to supervise the work of the house of the LORD.

What did Zerubbabel and Jeshua make?

Whom did they make a beginning with?

In Ezra 3, the Israelites had returned home. Two generations had passed since they last saw their homeland. They had been taken in the midst of a raid (see Jer. 52:12–30), and the scene they walked into was more than just a mess that could be taken care of in an afternoon. They faced a long, hard road to recovery.

Try to imagine this scene of rubble and destruction. Consider the weight of the scope of the work that lay before them. Where would you begin? What would you do first?

We might assume the Israelites got to the work of rebuilding the city immediately, but they didn't. As we anticipate the rebuilding of the nation of Israel, we see a different first step. Read Ezra 3:1–3:

> When the seventh month came, and the children of Israel were in the towns, the people gathered as one man to Jerusalem. Then arose Jeshua the son of Jozadak, with his fellow priests, and Zerubbabel the son of Shealtiel with his kinsmen, and they built the altar of the God of Israel, to offer burnt offerings on it, as it is written in the Law of Moses the man of God. They set the altar in its place, for fear was on them because of the peoples of the lands, and they offered burnt offerings on it to the LORD, burnt offerings morning and evening.

According to these verses, what was the first thing they built?

Why did they build the altar?

Before the children of Israel did anything else, they built an altar. Not just any altar but the altar of the God of Israel. The altar signaled not only the nation's return to their homeland but also a return to their Lord. Throughout their history, two very important things would happen at the altar of the God of Israel.

1. At the altar, the people received God's forgiveness (see Lev. 4).
2. At the altar, the people prepared themselves for God's future purposes (see Ex. 19:10; Josh. 3:5).

Surrounded by the vast scope of work still to be done and their lack of resources to do it, God's people offered burnt offerings morning and evening and observed the regular feasts. The priority they placed on building the altar proved their commitment to pay careful attention to God's words to live set apart as holy to Him. It also demonstrated their dependence on God as their provider and protector. Then, only after restoring their relationship with God did they make a beginning to the other repairs.

Their work *for* the Lord followed their worship *of* Him. Many scholars believe that to set the altar in its place, the returning Israelites would have had to destroy an altar that had been built on that spot by the remaining inhabitants of the land.[1]

As we begin the final week of our study on belonging, what has God revealed to you that is broken and in need of restoration in your life?

What do you need to tear down in order to let God's blessing of belonging begin in your life?

Maybe today you're facing a broken relationship or a sin pattern you can't seem to break. I hope you're ready to get to work restoring what's been lost. While you may be willing to jump right into the work, our starting line for every beginning is Jesus. Belonging never begins with what we can do for God; it always begins with what He's already done for us.

Jesus is our altar (see Heb. 13:10). He is the source of our personal forgiveness, and it is only in the steadfast love of God through Christ that we find victory.

> *Belonging never begins with what we can do for God; it always begins with what He's already done for us.*

For God's people, there was an exciting beginning to be made, but the road ahead would not be easy. Israel faced years of restoration work as they rebuilt the temple and their homeland. This week, we will walk with them as they encounter opposition, discouragement, and doubt. What we'll learn is that our road to belonging is no different. While the beginning is exciting and can hold great promise, the reality of restoration work is hard. In order to rebuild and see the work to completion, we must come first and frequently to the altar, the head of the body, Jesus Christ.

WORK IT OUT

Each day this week in the "Work It Out" section, you will find a prayer. Use the prayer as a starting point. Personalize it to reflect your heart and the things God brings to your attention.

It may feel easier to skim past this section and move on, but as we've learned today, the belonging we yearn for begins at the altar of Christ. Bring your brokenness to Jesus, and let Him heal you and lead you to a new start. To slow yourself down, say the words below out loud; then write them down in your own prayer journal.

Dear God,

As I survey the reality of the rubble in my life, I know there is no hope outside of Jesus. Forgive me for thinking I can rebuild anything apart from You. Today, I come to the altar of Christ and offer up a sacrifice of praise to You.

In Jesus' name, amen.

Day 2

The First Step to Doing Your Part

Memory Verse

I am sure of this, that he who started a _____

_____ in you will carry it on to

completion until the day of Christ Jesus.

Philippians 1:6 CSB

"Don't squeeze," the teacher instructed. "Just kind of sink all the way to the bottom."

As she taught her eager students to play new notes, my sons' violin teacher noticed they took their effort a little too far. They focused hard and fixed their eyes on the strings. They wanted so badly to do it right, but their work didn't produce the results they'd hoped for. The notes screeched off the strings, and the sound pierced the air, forced and harsh.

My boys looked confused. They'd tried so hard, and it just wasn't working. *What did I do wrong?* they wondered.

That's when the music teacher loosened their grip. "Sink, don't squeeze," she said. "The note will play itself. Simply place your finger on the string, and let it sink all the way down."

When my boys were in their first years of violin lessons, as they tried hard to play the right notes the right way, their grip on the strings would tighten, causing the sound to slice through the air in a not-so-pleasant way. The teacher corrected this habit by encouraging them to loosen their grip and simply let their fingers sink into the strings instead of squeezing them. When they did, the sound played just as they had hoped.

As we continue our journey with Israel, we'll discover the difference between relying on ourselves to accomplish God's plans and simply sinking into God's purposes. Before we go any further, let's review what we learned in week 2 of our study.

Read Ephesians 4:4–6: "There is one body and one Spirit—just as you were called to the one hope that belongs to your call—one Lord, one faith, one baptism, one God and Father of all, who is over all and through all and in all." Week 2 taught us we are not only called *to* One, but we are also called to *be one*. We learned that belonging brings oneness, and as one body we are called to contend both *for* something and *against* someone.

On our journey with the nation of Israel and the rebuilding of their homeland, we now move to the book of the Bible that introduces us to Nehemiah, an Israelite living in captivity in Babylon.

DIGGING IN

Read Nehemiah 2:1–2:

> In the month of Nisan, in the twentieth year of King Artaxerxes, when wine was before him, I took up the wine and gave it to the king. Now I had not been sad in his presence. And the king said to me, "Why is your face sad, seeing you are not sick? This is nothing but sadness of the heart." Then I was very much afraid.

These verses give us some important details about our journey with the nation of Israel. What month was it?

Where was Nehemiah?

How did King Artaxerxes identify Nehemiah's condition?

How did Nehemiah feel when the king pointed out his sadness of heart?

Nehemiah's face didn't tell a story of physical sickness. Instead, it was a story of heart sickness—a heart sickness that infected him so deeply it had to be dealt with. To find out why Nehemiah's face showed this sadness of heart, we need to go back to chapter 1.

Read Nehemiah 1:1–3:

> The words of Nehemiah the son of Hacaliah. Now it happened in the month of Chislev, in the twentieth year, as I was in Susa the citadel, that Hanani, one of my brothers, came with certain men from Judah. And I asked them concerning the Jews who escaped, who had survived the exile, and concerning Jerusalem. And they said to me, "The remnant there in the province who had survived the exile is in great trouble and shame. The wall of Jerusalem is broken down, and its gates are destroyed by fire."

In these verses, what month is it?

Where is Nehemiah?

What does Nehemiah ask the men who came from Judah?

How do they describe the scene in Judah?

As the book of Nehemiah opens, we find Nehemiah inquiring of his kinsman about the Jews who are in Jerusalem. Their answer includes words like *trouble*, *shame*, *broken*, *destroyed*. To paraphrase: "It's bad, Nehemiah. It's really bad."

The remaining verses of chapter 1 record Nehemiah's grief and prayer in the wake of this news. Though Nehemiah hadn't been with his kinsman in Jerusalem, he nevertheless belonged to the nation of Israel, so he mourned the condition of his homeland. So much so that the sadness of his heart moved him to take risks and take action.

In spite of where he lived and his position in the king's court, Nehemiah knew he belonged to God and the people of God. Because he knew where he belonged, Nehemiah's heart was available to be used by God.

As we consider Nehemiah's example, we can draw from three things to help us prepare our hearts to be used by God in the body of Christ. First, **a heart that knows where it belongs is willing to be broken.** From Chislev to Nisan, Nehemiah mainly spent his time mourning, fasting, and praying. That's about a four-month span of sadness.[1] Nehemiah allowed his heart to not just be bothered by the despair of God's people but to also be broken by it.

Sometimes it's easier to acknowledge a problem and even pray about a problem, all the while keeping our distance. The troubles of this world can feel desperate and overwhelming, but a heart that is willing to be broken over the things that break God's heart is a heart that is available to be used by God.

What would it look like for you to have a heart that is willing to be broken by things that break God's heart, especially as it pertains to the body of Christ?

Next, **a heart that knows where it belongs is willing to be moved**. Ancient customs prohibited anyone from being sad in the royal court.[2] By all accounts, Nehemiah made up his mind to let his broken heart be seen by the king (see Neh. 1:11), thus risking being rejected or even killed. So it was a really big deal that Nehemiah let the king see his sadness.

Nehemiah's broken heart led him into bold action. He didn't just bring the troubles of God's people to the king's attention; he took it one step further. Read Nehemiah 2:5: "I said to the king, 'If it pleases the king, and if your servant has found favor in your sight, that you send me to Judah, to the city of my fathers' graves, that I may rebuild it.'"

What did Nehemiah ask the king to do?

Why did he ask the king to send him to Judah?

As cupbearer to the king, Nehemiah held a high position that would have provided him comfort and honor.[3] Remember the condition of Judah as it was described by his kinsman? Those conditions would have been very different from the ones Nehemiah currently lived in, yet he was willing to trade all of it for an eight-hundred-mile journey to a city in ruins. His choice would not have been the most pleasurable one, nor the easiest. But because Nehemiah belonged to the community of Israel, his heart was willing to be moved for the sake of accomplishing God's work, specifically for rebuilding the walls of Jerusalem.

What would it look like for you to be willing to be moved by Christ because you belong to the body of Christ?

Finally, **a heart that knows where it belongs is willing to believe God.** The thread that pulls all the way through the books of Ezra and Nehemiah is the good hand of God. Look up the verses below, and connect them to what they say about the good and gracious hand of God.

Ezra 7:9	delivered the people from their enemies
Ezra 8:31	gave Nehemiah favor in the sight of the king
Nehemiah 2:8	encouraged the people in Jerusalem to begin the work of rebuilding
Nehemiah 2:18	guided Ezra safely from Babylon to Jerusalem

We can trace a line of trust in God through each step Nehemiah took on the road to restoration in Jerusalem. Nehemiah trusted God to open the door before King Artaxerxes. He trusted God to move the king's heart as he made his request. Despite the scale of the work and open opposition to it (we'll talk more about this tomorrow), Nehemiah believed God would carry the work of rebuilding the walls of Jerusalem to completion (see 2:17–18).

Every step Nehemiah took was a step of dependence on God, not on himself. Like my sons and their violins, I can sometimes be willing to respond to God's calling, but I try so hard to carry out the mission with my own strength and ability that I end up squeezing out God's purposes instead of sinking into them.

We must let our identity in Christ and in the body of Christ to which we belong be catalysts that soften our hearts to each other and prepare us for God's purposes.

We may not be commissioned to do work like Nehemiah's, but because we belong to Jesus, we are all called to participate in God's purposes. We must let our identity in Christ and in the body of Christ to which we belong be catalysts that soften our hearts to each other and prepare us for God's purposes.

WORK IT OUT

Review the three signs of a heart that knows where it belongs:

1. A heart that knows where it belongs is willing to be broken.
2. A heart that knows where it belongs is willing to be moved.
3. A heart that knows where it belongs is willing to believe God.

Which one of these three signs do you find most challenging?

How can you bring this to God and allow Him to shape your heart?

Say the words of the prayer below out loud; then write this prayer using your own words in a prayer journal.

Dear God,

Give me a heart willing to be broken by the things that break Your heart. Send me to share Your hope and love with others! As I go, give me a heart that trusts You to do what only You can do.

In Jesus' name, amen.

Day 3

When the Enemy Attacks, Do This

Memory Verse

I am sure of this, that he who started a _____ _____ *in*

you will carry it on to _____ *until the day of Christ Jesus.*

Philippians 1:6 CSB

We couldn't believe our eyes.

In the darkness of the night, we pulled up to our house after our son's basketball game, and there it was in the middle of the driveway. "A copperhead!" one of our children exclaimed from the back seat.

At the moment of our child's announcement, I couldn't see what he saw, but based on the reaction of everyone else in the car, I believed him. I drove a little farther and, sure enough, I saw what looked like a snake coiled up in the middle of our driveway.

Since none of us were willing to get out of the car while the unwelcome reptile rested nearby, my only option was to try to run over the snake from the safety of the vehicle. Tightly gripping the wheel, I steered the car according to the directions I received from the rest of the group.

Luke sat next to me in the passenger seat while the kids shouted instructions from the back. With one voice they would call out, "Right! Left! Straight!" Collectively, we worked to defeat the foe in the driveway that night. We didn't really have a choice … because no one was getting out of that car until we did.

The good news is, the snake didn't get us. It is not, however, because we successfully defeated the snake.

As we inched nearer and nearer to the enemy in the driveway and tried to strategically run over it with the wheel—any wheel—of the car, we discovered it wasn't actually a snake at all.

It was a leaf, which was not nearly as threatening as the aforementioned copperhead we had believed it to be.

In our defense, it was dark. Who knew a leaf could look so much like a snake coiled up, lying in wait for an unsuspecting family to return home?

We've learned through the course of our study that as one body in Christ we are called to contend both *for* something and *against* someone. We have a common enemy, and it's definitely not a leaf in the driveway.

Let's review what we learned about our common enemy in week 2. Read John 17:14–15: "I have given them your word, and the world has hated them because they are not of the world, just as I am not of the world. I do not ask that you take them out of the world, but that you keep them from the evil one." In these verses, Jesus identified two enemies of His followers: the world and the Evil One.

Today, as we continue our journey with the nation of Israel and their quest to rebuild the wall of Jerusalem, we will see them encounter a physical enemy and learn some practical ways that we too can respond in the face of our common enemy.

DIGGING IN

Read Nehemiah 2:9–10:

> Then I came to the governors of the province Beyond the River and gave them the king's letters. Now the king had sent with me officers of the army and horsemen. But when Sanballat the Horonite and Tobiah the Ammonite servant heard this, it displeased them greatly that someone had come to seek the welfare of the people of Israel.

What two names follow the word *But?*

Why were Sanballat the Horonite and Tobiah the Ammonite displeased?

As I read verse 10, my mind hears the sound of an ominous tune that goes something like *Duh-duh-duh.* At this point, Nehemiah had not even arrived in Jerusalem, but his enemies already knew of his intentions. Sanballat is believed to have been the governor of Samaria at the time, and Tobiah is believed to have been the governor of the Ammonites. A few verses later in chapter 2, we see that by the time Nehemiah called the people to action and they began the work of rebuilding the wall, their enemies had increased and surrounded them on every side[1]—Samaria to the north, Ammon to the east, and Arabia to the south.

Read verses 19–20:

> But when Sanballat the Horonite and Tobiah the Ammonite servant and Geshem the Arab heard of it, they jeered at us and despised us and said, "What is this thing that you are doing? Are you rebelling against the king?" Then I replied to them, "The God of heaven will make us prosper, and we his servants will arise and build, but you have no portion or right or claim in Jerusalem."

Here we have the word *But* again. It seems that with every step Nehemiah took toward uniting God's people to accomplish God's purposes, the enemy also took a step to attack.

Verse 19 adds another name to the list of the enemies. What is that name?

What did the enemies do?

What did they say?

The enemy voices questioned the Israelites' motives and threatened them with false accusations. In doing so, the enemies sought to create doubt and fear in the hearts of God's people. Nehemiah, however, did not shrink back in the face of the enemy. Record Nehemiah's answer to the enemies' question here:

Verse 20 details his response, which includes four very important points:

1. Nehemiah answered the enemies' accusations with the truth.
2. Nehemiah acknowledged his position as a servant of God and God as the one who would make the Israelites successful.
3. Nehemiah committed to obeying God in spite of their enemies' opposition.
4. Nehemiah identified them as having no part in Jerusalem's past, present, or future.

Just as we learned that our starting point for belonging is the altar of Christ, so also the starting point for Nehemiah's response to the enemy was God and what He would do. After speaking the truth about who God is and what He would do, Nehemiah spoke the truth about who he was and what he and God's people would accomplish because of God. Finally,

Nehemiah pointed out that as enemies of God, these accusers had no part or place in the city or its affairs.

Because we belong to Jesus, we share a common enemy. Our enemy has employed the same tactics used against God's people in the book of Nehemiah from the beginning of time until now.

Look up and read Genesis 3:1–5 and Matthew 4:1–11; then answer the following:

What question did the enemy ask Eve?

What questions did the enemy ask Jesus?

Where do you see the tactic of creating fear, doubt, or confusion in each scene?

In the garden of Eden with Eve and in the wilderness with Jesus, Satan used the same tactic of creating fear, doubt, and confusion. Eve and Jesus, however, responded very differently. While Eve entertained the serpent's words and gave in to the doubt and confusion he created (see Gen. 3:6), Jesus answered the Devil with the truth of God's Word.

As Jesus combatted the Devil with truth in the wilderness, Nehemiah also silenced his enemies with truth. And despite the enemies' attempts to halt the work of the Lord, Nehemiah and those in Jerusalem began to rebuild the walls around the city. Their work would strengthen the city and protect it. Instead of desolate, it would be inhabited. Instead of ruined, it would be rebuilt.

In order to accomplish this, though, it would take everyone. Nehemiah 3 is a chapter with a lot of hard-to-pronounce names and a lot of places you are probably not familiar with. I don't want to skip over it, though. When you come to a name you can't pronounce, try it anyway, or you can do what my kids do and just say the first letter of the word. So verse 1 would sound something like this: "Then E the high priest rose up with his brothers the priests, and they built the Sheep Gate.... They consecrated it as far as the Tower of the Hundred, as far as the Tower of H." You get the idea.

Open your Bible and read Nehemiah 3.

Verses 2, 4, and 5 all begin with the same phrase. What is it?

This chapter records the phrase "next to him/them" fifteen times. Beginning in verse 16 there is a shift to a similar phrase—"after him"—a phrase used thirteen more times. If you're keeping count, that's nearly thirty times this chapter uses the phrase "next to him" or "after him."

The work could not be done by any one person alone. The picture Nehemiah 3 paints is of a shoulder-to-shoulder effort in which one community, united under one Lord, worked together as one against a common enemy for the sake of the common good. These workers were priests, goldsmiths, perfumers, temple servants, and rulers from different cities and households, all repairing and rebuilding different parts of the wall.

Despite their shared enemy, their common identity united them in a common bond. Because of this common bond, they strove side by side for the sake of their work for the Lord. Because they worked together, they did not have to face their enemy alone.

Read Nehemiah 4:7–9:

> But when Sanballat and Tobiah and the Arabs and the Ammonites and the Ashdodites heard that the repairing of the walls of Jerusalem was going forward and that the breaches were beginning to be closed, they were very

angry. And they all plotted together to come and fight against Jerusalem and to cause confusion in it. And we prayed to our God and set a guard as a protection against them day and night.

Duh-duh-duh. Here we go again. As you might expect, we again have the word *But*, and once again, the list of enemies against God's people has grown. The familiar foes Sanballat and Tobiah, along with Arabs, are now joined by the Ashdodites. News that repair of the walls was going forward made them anxious and angry and caused them to join forces against the work of the Lord.

According to the last sentence of these verses, the Jews did two things in response to the enemy threats. What did they do?

We too will encounter opposition as we seek to carry out God's will, and we too can stand firm in the face of our enemy. Armed with the truth (see Eph. 6:14), we can follow Jesus' example and answer the enemy with the truth. Then we can choose to obey God, counting on His power, His strength, and His plan.

When we work together, we do not have to face our enemy alone. Like Nehemiah and God's people, in the face of our enemy we can come together, pray, and hold tightly to the unity of the Spirit in the bond of peace.

Because we belong to Jesus, we can live whole no matter what we face, and we can advance together for the cause of Christ.

WORK IT OUT

As we acknowledge the reality of a common enemy and study the tactics he employs to deceive us, confuse us, and make us afraid, I can think of no better time to remember the bond of peace given to us through Jesus. As we learned in week 3, this peace is a peace we can't find apart from Christ. It's a peace that is so much more than quiet circumstances. This peace is God's gift of wholeness to His people.

Because we've focused so much on our enemy, I want to end today by remembering our bond of peace. Because we belong to Jesus, we can live whole no matter what we face, and we can advance together for the cause of Christ. Say the prayer below aloud if you can, or write it out. Feel free to use some of your own words as you do.

> Dear God,
> I want the peace of Christ to rule in my heart. Show me the places where I seek peace apart from the company of Christ. Give me the courage to lean on You and press into the body of Christ.
> In Jesus' name, amen.

Day 4

Compelled to Continue, Together

Memory Verse

I am sure of this, that he who started a _____

_____ in you will _____ _____ _____

to _____ until the day of Christ Jesus.

Philippians 1:6 CSB

I told everyone I knew.

I drove all over town to tell people. Those I couldn't tell in person, I called on the phone. The man of my dreams had just asked me to marry him, and I wanted the whole world to hear the good news!

Over the next several weeks, Luke and I planned and looked forward to the wedding day. That day, when it finally came, was everything I could have asked for, and it still makes me smile when I remember it.

But shortly after that day, the pomp and circumstance quieted. The crowds went back to their normal lives. No one called to celebrate or plan. Our marriage was no longer an event; it was a life.

We've come to an exciting moment in our restoration journey with Israel. Today, we will walk with them as they complete the work. Quite possibly, they finished the job in record time. What happened next may surprise you, but before we go any further, let's do a quick review of what we studied last week.

Read Ephesians 4:11–14:

> He gave the apostles, the prophets, the evangelists, the shepherds and teach-
> ers, to equip the saints for the work of ministry, for building up the body of
> Christ, until we all attain to the unity of the faith and of the knowledge of
> the Son of God, to mature manhood, to the measure of the stature of the
> fullness of Christ, so that we may no longer be children, tossed to and fro by
> the waves and carried about by every wind of doctrine, by human cunning,
> by craftiness in deceitful schemes.

We have a common goal that compels us to continue together. As we use our gifts to build
up the body of Christ in love, we grow to a spiritual maturity that exemplifies the character of
Jesus. Sometimes, our common goal requires sacrifice, but to attain the measure of the stature
of the fullness of Christ, we must continually cultivate spiritual growth and create conditions
ripe for Jesus to bring it to completion.

I'm on the edge of my seat! Let's see how this story ends.

DIGGING IN

Read Nehemiah 6:15–16:

> So the wall was finished on the twenty-fifth day of the month Elul, in fifty-
> two days. And when all our enemies heard of it, all the nations around us
> were afraid and fell greatly in their own esteem, for they perceived that this
> work had been accomplished with the help of our God.

How many days did it take to finish the wall?

What happened to their enemies when they heard the wall was finished?

Why were they afraid?

Here it is! The moment our journey has been leading to. God turned the tables so that in spite of their enemies' continued threats, it was those enemies who were afraid when the wall was finished.

The fact that this project went from start to finish in a matter of fifty-two days is remarkable. In less than two months' time, a wall—which had been broken, ruined, and destroyed—stood tall, sturdy, and strong.

The achievement is so remarkable, in fact, that Jewish historian Josephus questioned how realistic this timeline would have been, and he even went so far as to change his record of the timing to reflect a much longer build.[1] Scholars agree, however, that we have no reason to question the Bible's record of how long it took to build the walls because, as Nehemiah noted, the work was accomplished with the help of God.[2]

The Jews had labored together, struggled together, trembled together, and persevered together. This seems like a happy ending to the story—a good stopping point—but believe it or not, there was more work to do.

The next several chapters detail Nehemiah's appointment of officers who would make sure the city functioned properly and further detail how the entire community repented and recommitted themselves to worship and serve the Lord. As Nehemiah 11 begins, the temple—the place of God's presence—has been restored and the walls of Jerusalem—a symbol of God's protection—have been rebuilt. Now it's time to live in the city.

The current condition of the city was spacious but empty (see 7:4). To leave the city as it was would be to leave it vulnerable and ultimately purposeless. Even with the work of the wall complete, the children of God needed to continue.

Read Nehemiah 11:1–2:

> The leaders of the people lived in Jerusalem. And the rest of the people cast lots to bring one out of ten to live in Jerusalem the holy city, while nine out of ten remained in the other towns. And the people blessed all the men who willingly offered to live in Jerusalem.

Who lived in Jerusalem?

What did the rest of the people do to determine who would live in Jerusalem?

By all accounts, there wasn't a Black-Friday-like mob waiting at the Sheep Gate and hoping to be the first to live in the city. Instead, we read about the selection process of casting lots. People had to be picked to live in the city. It seems a little surprising that more weren't eager to enjoy life behind the walls, but a closer look exposes some of the reasons they might have hesitated.

To live in Jerusalem would be to face risk. God's people knew well the opposition that had surrounded them while they'd rebuilt the city walls, and they knew Jerusalem would remain a target of opposition.

To live in Jerusalem would also require more work. Few people lived in Jerusalem, and the houses inside the city had not yet been rebuilt (see 7:4). To remain in the city would mean more rebuilding.

Finally, to remain in the city of Jerusalem would require reimagining the future. The people had their own property in the surrounding towns. To live in Jerusalem would mean surrendering their former plans in favor of God's new plan.

I imagine the people were tired from the work they'd already done. I can only assume they desired some amount of certainty and comfort. Can you blame them? Yet to truly see this work to completion, they needed to continue … together.

In Philippians 2, Paul tells the Christians in Philippi to "work out your own salvation with fear and trembling" (v. 12b). The Amplified Bible translates it, "continue to work out your salvation [that is, cultivate it, bring it to full effect, actively pursue spiritual maturity]." That's what God's people needed to do inside the holy city: cultivate it and bring it to full effect. That's what we too must do as members of the body of Christ.

Similar to my wedding day, salvation is not merely a one-day event in our lives. We don't just get saved and go home. As we live every day in Christ, we continue to work out our salvation. We cultivate it daily. We come together in the body of Christ to pursue growth and build each other up in love. As we do, we will experience a life of belonging—full of peace, security, and purpose.

WORK IT OUT

Of the three things listed in today's study that caused God's people to hesitate to live in Jerusalem (risk, rebuilding, reimagining the future), which one is most likely to make you hesitate in pursuing growth in the body of Christ?

As we draw near to the end of our study on belonging in the body of Christ, I wonder if God is calling you closer to Himself and His body. Maybe you're tired and don't really want to continue to cultivate growth in the body of Christ. Maybe you had plans that would require some reimagining in order to prioritize growing in Christ and in His body. If that's you, I want to remind you: the body of Christ is not only an essential piece of *your* belonging, but *you* are also an essential part of the body of Christ.

Several years ago, my pastor challenged us with two questions: "What do you have?" and "What will you do with it?" As we learn to continue to work out our salvation, say the prayer below out loud; then ask God to help you answer these questions.

Dear God,

Reveal to me what You have given me and how You want me to use it to accomplish Your purposes. Forgive me for my hesitation when You lead me to places that feel risky or uncertain. I want to daily cultivate my relationship with You and grow from fine to flourishing in the body of Christ.

In Jesus' name, amen.

Day 5

Do It Together: Give Thanks

Memory Verse

I am sure of this, that he who _____ a _____

_____ in you will _____ _____ _____

to _____ until the day of Christ Jesus.

Philippians 1:6 CSB

There I was, on the back row of the church again. And crying, again.

This time, though, the tears weren't from sadness or loneliness. Instead, they were from an overflow of gratitude for what God had done. Almost a year before this moment, I had crawled into my bed with tears in my eyes. I had learned that the life of the baby in my womb was severely threatened by a hemorrhage and the only way to preserve his life was to be on bed rest for several months. We scrambled to make arrangements for the care of our other children, and I helplessly laid in my bed, praying for the life of our unborn child.

As time went on, he grew and strengthened, and on the day of his birth, he weighed in as the heaviest child we'd had.

That day on the back row of the church came five months after his birth. It occurred to me in that moment all that God had brought us through, how He had answered our prayers, and that up until that point, I had never paused to thank Him. I had kept going, moving from one thing to the next. I had been so busy doing the next thing that I hadn't paused to give thanks.

I think when we give thanks *together*, we find the dividing walls between us coming down. When we're focused on all God has done for us and given to us, we find it more difficult to complain or hold on to an offense.

Paul addresses this in his letter to the Ephesians. As he continues his teaching on how to walk in a manner worthy of the calling of Christ, Paul wrote:

> Ever be filled and stimulated with the [Holy] Spirit. Speak out to one another in psalms and hymns and spiritual songs, offering praise with voices [and instruments] and making melody with all your heart to the Lord, At all times and for everything giving thanks in the name of our Lord Jesus Christ to God the Father. (5:18b–20 AMPC)

There's so much life in these verses. The attitude of my heart is especially lifted by these phrases: "be filled … with the Holy Spirit," "speak out to one another in psalms and hymns and spiritual songs," "praise … and making melody with all your heart to the Lord," and "at all times and for everything giving thanks."

Paul echoed this sentiment in his letter to another early church when he wrote, "Give thanks in everything, for this is God's will for you in Christ Jesus" (1 Thess. 5:18 HCSB).

In both letters, Paul urges early Christians to give thanks at all times and in everything. You may have noticed some familiar words at the end of the verse in 1 Thessalonians. Paul's reason for this call to give thanks is because it's "God's will for you in Christ Jesus."

As we close our study together, this reminds me of where we began. Because we are in Christ, we belong to the body of Christ. Because we belong to Jesus, we have reason to give thanks at all times and for everything. While it may be easier to recount the wrongs that have been done to us or to go into a tailspin in the midst of the problems we face, God's Word reminds us to give thanks.

Let's not miss an opportunity to give thanks together. The next time you open your mouth in the company of others, remember the gift of gratitude.

WORK IT OUT

At the end of this week's study, you'll find a resource titled "The Path to Belonging." This resource details the four steps we've discussed this week and how they relate to everything you've learned throughout this entire study. Review this resource; then come back here and answer the questions below.

Where are you on the path to belonging?

What step do you need to take today to move toward a life of belonging?

As we conclude our study together, go back to the "Work It Out" sections from the previous days and weeks. Is there anything you need to spend more time in prayer about? Is there an action you need to take in order to pursue belonging in the body of Christ? Remember what you've learned, and consider what has impacted you and how God has changed you through this journey.

Use the space below to give thanks to God for what He's done and what He will continue to do as you live a life that belongs in Christ and in His body.

_____

_____

_____

_____

_____

_____

_____

_____

The Path to Belonging

Begin

BELONGING BEGINS IN THE MIDST OF OUR BROKENNESS.

"He himself bore our sins in his body on the tree, that we might die to sin and live to righteousness. By his wounds you have been healed." (1 Pet. 2:24)

BELONGING BRINGS ONENESS.

"Holy Father, keep them in your name, which you have given me, that they may be one, even as we are one." (John 17:11b)

Come Together

Work Together

BELONGING BESTOWS THE BOND OF PEACE.

"Make every effort to keep the oneness of the Spirit in the bond of peace [each individual working together to make the whole successful]." (Eph. 4:3 AMP)

BELONGING CULTIVATES GROWTH THAT CAUSES US TO FLOURISH.

"It is love, then, that you should strive for. Set your hearts on spiritual gifts." (1 Cor. 14:1 GNT)

Grow Together

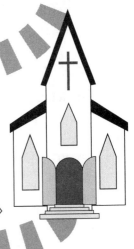

BELONGING PREPARES US FOR GOD'S PURPOSES.

"I am sure of this, that he who started a good work in you will carry it on to completion until the day of Christ Jesus." (Phil. 1:6 CSB)

Continue Together

Week 5 Group Time

Welcome

- Leader: Introduce week 5 by asking each member to share anything she underlined or highlighted.
- Review the memory verse for the week: Philippians 1:6.

Watch the week 5 video: "What Happens When We Belong."

Discussion Questions

- Read Ezra 3:1–3, and review the two things from day 1 that would happen at the altar of God. What has God revealed to you that is broken and in need of restoration?
- On day 2, read the three signs of a heart that knows where it belongs. Which one of these three do you find most challenging?
- Katy wrote, "When we work together, we do not have to face our enemy alone." How have you experienced this in your life?
- On day 4, Katy challenged us with two questions: "What do you have?" and "What will you do with it?" Share your answers.
- Turn to the resource called "The Path to Belonging." Read each step and the verse that goes along with it.
- Where are you on the path? What step do you need to take to move toward a life of belonging?

Close in Prayer

- Ask for prayer requests, and thank God for your time together.
- Ask God to help you take your place in the body of Christ.

Reminders for the Close of the Study

- Spend time reading the conclusion, and consider God's plan for His body.
- Skim the study guide, and complete any blanks you weren't ready to address on your first pass.
- When you're exhausted, overwhelmed, and consumed by life, remember the body of Christ is where you'll find peace, security, and purpose.

Conclusion

Grab a Balloon

I drove alone. Even the road seemed to be empty. My heavy heart was the only thing that accompanied me on this trip.

I was driving to an event where I would soon tell the women gathered in the room about how we needed each other and how God had designed us to live in community with one another, bearing with each other and building each other up. While I knew it was true in my mind, my heart felt only the sting of rejection.

I had recently sacrificed what felt like a lot in order to serve a group of fellow followers of Jesus. I had given time, money, tears, and physical toil toward something that ultimately seemed to go unnoticed and unappreciated. My heart hurt, and I was tempted to pull away.

As I squeezed the steering wheel and gritted my teeth to stay strong and get through this, the radio host on the airwaves told a story.

She set the scene of a college classroom where hundreds of students were given an assignment. The professor handed out an inflated balloon to every student with a simple instruction: write your name on the balloon. Next, the professor opened the door to the classroom and instructed every student to throw their balloon into the hallway. The balloons floated around for a while; then the experiment began.

The students were told to enter the hallway and find the balloon with their name on it. They had only five minutes to recover it. The door opened, and hundreds of students flooded a hallway filled with hundreds of balloons, all on the same quest to find the balloon that bore their name.

Five minutes came and went. Of the hundreds of students hunting their balloons, not one found the right one. They filed back into the classroom, I'm sure a little dejected, while the balloons continued to float aimlessly in the hallway.

Next, the professor gave a different directive. Into the hallway they would go again, and again they would each hunt for a balloon. But this time, instead of finding the balloon with their name on it, the students were instructed to find *any* balloon with *any* name and return that balloon to the person to whom it belonged.

For the second time, hundreds of students flooded into a hallway filled with hundreds of balloons floating to and fro. But this time, with their new mission in mind, every student found a balloon. Each returned it to the person to whom it belonged, and in five minutes, every student held the balloon on which their name was written.

As I drove along the lonely road and considered the story told on the radio that day, I realized part of my problem was that I was out in the hall looking for my own balloon. My approach to life—to the burdens of each day—was more of an every-woman-for-herself attitude, and consequently, I felt anxious, aimless, and alone. My quest to keep it together had brought me dangerously close to falling apart.

Something began to shift for me that day. The words I knew to be true became more than "supposed tos" written in God's Word—they became desires of my heart. I began to understand that God's plan for His body is not for it to be endured but enjoyed.

Over the last five weeks, you've learned that to experience the fullness of belonging to the body of Christ, you need to:

- shift your identity from your scars to your Savior,
- put down your own ways so you can pull together with others for the cause of Christ,
- press into the body of Christ instead of pulling away from it—especially when life falls apart—and
- cultivate conditions that grow you from "fine" to flourishing.

I pray that you have begun to understand that finding your place in the body of Christ isn't meant to be a burden. Instead, it's what you've been created for—and called to—in Christ.

In the days ahead, as you seek to live a life of belonging in the body of Christ, I pray you'll remember what I learned that day in the car. Our quest to keep it together by ourselves will eventually cause us to fall apart. You don't have to do it on your own. When you're exhausted, overwhelmed, and consumed by life, remember the place where you'll find peace, security, and purpose.

Then grab a balloon—any balloon—and start living a life that belongs in the body of Christ.

I began to understand that God's plan for His body is not for it to be endured but enjoyed.

Reflections on Belonging

INTRODUCTION: I'VE GOT THIS

1. Alexa Lardieri, "Study: Many Americans Report Feeling Lonely, Younger Generations More So," *US News*, May 1, 2018, www.usnews.com/news/health-care-news/articles/2018–05–01/study-many-americans-report -feeling-lonely-younger-generations-more-so.

2. "One in Three Practicing Christians Has Stopped Attending Church During COVID-19," Barna: State of the Church, July 8, 2020, www.barna.com/research/new-sunday-morning-part-2.

3. "Friendships: Enrich Your Life and Improve Your Health," Mayo Clinic, January 12, 2022, www.mayoclinic.org/healthy-lifestyle/adult-health/in-depth/friendships/art-20044860.

WEEK 1, DAY 1: A PLACE FOR YOUR BROKEN PIECES

1. "Sense of Belonging," Cornell University, accessed September 27, 2022, https://diversity.cornell. edu/belonging/sense-belonging.

2. "H2938—ṭāʿam," Strong's Concordance, Blue Letter Bible, accessed April 12, 2022, www.blueletterbible.org /lexicon/h2938/esv/wlc/0–1.

3. Psalm 34:18 AMP.

4. Lettie B. Cowman, *Streams in the Desert* (Los Angeles: Oriental Missionary Society, 1925), 298–99.

WEEK 1, DAY 2: WHEN YOU DON'T FEEL ACCEPTED

1. "What Is the Significance of the Hem of Jesus' Garment?," End of the Matter, September 12, 2021, https://endofthematter.com/2015/10/why-is-there-healing-in-the-hem-of-jesus-garment.

2. Craig S. Keener, *Matthew, The IVP New Testament Commentary Series*, vol. 1, (Downers Grove, IL: InterVarsity Press, 1997), Matthew 9:18–26.

WEEK 1, DAY 3: FIXING IT ALL

1. Paul David Tripp, *New Morning Mercies: A Daily Gospel Devotional* (Wheaton, IL: Crossway, 2014), April 11.

WEEK 1, DAY 4: RESPOND TO YOUR CALLING

1. W. Barclay, *The Acts of the Apostles*, 3rd rev. ed. (Louisville, KY: John Knox, 2003), 114–115.

2. Robert W. Wall, "Community: New Testament," *The Anchor Bible Dictionary*, ed. David Noel Freedman, (New York: Doubleday, 1992), 1109.

WEEK 2, DAY 1: A PART OF THE WHOLE

1. *Oxford Languages Dictionary*, quoted by Google, accessed March 21, 2022, https://languages.oup.com /google-dictionary-en.

2. *Merriam-Webster*, s.v. "member," accessed March 21, 2022, www.merriam-webster.com/dictionary/member.

3. Harold W. Hoehner, Philip W. Comfort, and Peter H. Davids, *Ephesians, Philippians, 1&2 Thessalonians, Colossians, Philemon*, Cornerstone Biblical Commentary, Philip W. Comfort, ed., vol. 16 (Carol Stream, IL: Tyndale House, 2008), 80–81.

4. John R. W. Stott, *The Message of Ephesians* (Downers Grove, IL: InterVarsity Press, 1979), 150.

5. Walter A. Elwell and Philip Wesley Comfort, eds., *Tyndale Bible Dictionary* (Wheaton, IL: Tyndale House, 2001), 1275.

6. Stott, *Message of Ephesians*, 150.

WEEK 2, DAY 2: WORDS TO NEVER FORGET

1. Ephesians 1:17; 2:18, 20; 3:14–17; 5:18–20.

2. A. Boyd Luter Jr., "Christ, Body of," *The Anchor Bible Dictionary*, ed. David Noel Freedman (New York: Doubleday, 1992), 922.

3. Aiden Wilson Tozer, *The Knowledge of the Holy* (New York: HarperCollins, 1961), 22.

4. Tozer, *Knowledge of the Holy*, 23.

5. "G5048—teleioō," Strong's Concordance, Blue Letter Bible, accessed June 15, 2022, www.blueletterbible.org /lexicon/g5048/kjv/tr/0-1.

WEEK 2, DAY 3: SOMETHING WORTH FIGHTING FOR

1. Robert W. Wall, "Community: New Testament," *The Anchor Bible Dictionary*, ed. David Noel Freedman (New York: Doubleday, 1992), 1106.

2. "G1864—epagōnizomai," Strong's Concordance, Blue Letter Bible, accessed April 20, 2022, www.blueletterbible.org/lexicon/g1864/esv/mgnt/0-1.

3. John R. W. Stott, *The Message of Ephesians* (Downers Grove, IL: InterVarsity Press, 1979), 276.

4. Andrew Knowles, *The Bible Guide* (Minneapolis: Augsburg, 2001), 622.

5. "What Is the Shield of Faith (Ephesians 6:16)?," Got Questions, accessed June 14, 2022, www.gotquestions.org/shield-of-faith.html.

6. Walter L. Liefeld, *Ephesians, The IVP New Testament Commentary*, vol. 10 (Downers Grove, IL: InterVarsity Press, 1997), Ephesians 6:13–17.

WEEK 2, DAY 4: WHAT IF I GET HURT?

1. "G5083—tēreō," Strong's Concordance, Blue Letter Bible, accessed June 19, 2022, www.blueletterbible.org /lexicon/g5083/esv/mgnt/0-1.

2. "Paul's First Missionary Journey," BibleCharts.org, accessed June 14, 2022, www.biblecharts.org /apostlepaulcharts/5%20-%20Pauls%20First%20Missionary%20Journey.pdf.

3. "When Division Becomes Multiplication (Acts 15:3—16:10)," Bible.org, accessed March 23, 2022, https://bible.org/seriespage/24-when-division-becomes-multiplication-acts-153-1610 33.

4. John 21:19; Matthew 4:19.

WEEK 3, DAY 1: WHEN YOU FEEL LIKE YOU'RE FALLING APART

1. "1515.eirếnē," HELPS Word-studies, Bible Hub, accessed March 28, 2022, https://biblehub.com/greek/1515.htm.

WEEK 3, DAY 2: FOLLOWING THE STEPS OF WHOLENESS

1. Craig S. Keener, *The IVP Bible Background Commentary: New Testament* (Downers Grove, IL: InterVarsity Press, 1993), John 13:3–8.

2. John R. W. Stott, *The Message of Ephesians* (Downers Grove, IL: InterVarsity Press, 1979), 148.

WEEK 3, DAY 3: THE ENEMY OF BELONGING

1. John R. W. Stott, *The Message of Ephesians* (Downers Grove, IL: InterVarsity Press, 1979), 148.

2. Douglas K. Stuart, *Exodus*, The New American Commentary, E. Ray Clendenen, ed., vol. 2 (Nashville: Broadman & Holman, 2006), 239.

3. "Strong's G769—astheneia," Blue Letter Bible, accessed October 25, 2022, www.blueletterbible.org/lexicon /g769/esv/mgnt/0-1.

4. Elliot Ritzema and Elizabeth Vince, eds., *300 Quotations for Preachers from the Puritans*, Pastorum Series (Bellingham, WA: Lexham, 2013).

WEEK 3, DAY 4: KEEP DOING THIS

1. Jennifer Gaeng, "Coyote Howling: Why Do Coyotes Make Sounds at Night?," AZ Animals, January 6, 2022, https://a-z-animals.com/blog/coyote-howling-why-do-coyotes-make-sounds-at-night.

2. Matthew L. Miller, "The Howling: Why You're Hearing Coyotes This Month," Cool Green Science, February 13, 2019, https://blog.nature.org/science/2019/02/13/the-howling-why-youre-hearing-coyotes-this-month.

3. Lettie B. Cowman, *Streams in the Desert* (Los Angeles: The Oriental Missionary Society, 1925), 363.

4. "Strong's G37—hagiazō," Blue Letter Bible, accessed April 21, 2022, www.blueletterbible.org/lexicon /g37/esv/mgnt/0-1.

WEEK 3, DAY 5: DO IT TOGETHER: MEET

1. "G3948—paroxysmos," Strong's Concordance, Blue Letter Bible, accessed March 29, 2022, www.blueletterbible.org/lexicon/g3948/esv/mgnt/0-1.

WEEK 4, DAY 1: THE MEASURE OF THE FULLNESS OF CHRIST

1. "G4138—plērōma," Strong's Concordance, Blue Letter Bible, accessed April 25, 2022, www.blueletterbible .org/lexicon/g4138/esv/mgnt/0-1.

2. "G4137—plēroō," Strong's Concordance, Blue Letter Bible, accessed April 25, 2022, www.blueletterbible .org/lexicon/g4137/esv/mgnt/0-1.

WEEK 4, DAY 2: CULTIVATING YOUR MOST COMPLETE LIFE

1. "G2722—katechō," Strong's Concordance, Blue Letter Bible, accessed April 26, 2022, www.blueletterbible .org/lexicon/g2722/esv/mgnt/0-1.

WEEK 4, DAY 3: LET US USE THEM

1. "G4851—sympherō," Strong's Concordance, Blue Letter Bible, accessed April 28, 2022, www.blueletterbible .org/lexicon/g4851/esv/mgnt/0-1.

2. Larry Gilbert, "How Many Spiritual Gifts Are There?," ChurchGrowth.org, accessed April 27, 2022, https://churchgrowth.org/how-many-spiritual-gifts-are-there.

3. John R. W. Stott, *The Message of Ephesians* (Downers Grove, IL: InterVarsity Press, 1979), 159.

4. "What Is the Difference between a Talent and Spiritual Gift?," Got Questions, accessed October 3, 2022, www.gotquestions.org/difference-talent-spiritual-gift.html.

WEEK 4, DAY 4: WHAT ARE YOU STRIVING FOR?

1. "G4550—sapros," Strong's Concordance, Blue Letter Bible, accessed October 3, 2022, www.blueletterbible .org/lexicon/g4550/esv/mgnt/0-1.

2. "G3054—logomacheō," Strong's Concordance, Blue Letter Bible, accessed April 28, 2022, www.blueletterbible.org/lexicon/g3054/esv/mgnt/0-1.

3. Joan E. Greve, "Who Talks More, Men or Women? The Answer Isn't as Obvious as You Think," *Time*, July 16, 2014, https://time.com/2992051/women-talk-more-study.

WEEK 5, DAY 1: READY FOR A NEW START

1. David Guzik, "Ezra 3—A Foundation for the New Temple," Enduring Word, accessed November 15, 2022, https://enduringword.com/bible-commentary/ezra-3.

WEEK 5, DAY 2: THE FIRST STEP TO DOING YOUR PART

1. Mervin Breneman, *Ezra, Nehemiah, Esther,* The New American Commentary, Mervin Breneman, ed., vol. 10 (Nashville: Broadman & Holman, 1993), 174.

2. John D. Barry et al., *Faithlife Study Bible* (Bellingham, WA: Lexham, 2016), Nehemiah 2:2.

3. John H. Walton, Victor Harold Matthews, and Mark W. Chavalas, *The IVP Bible Background Commentary: Old Testament* (Downers Grove, IL: InterVarsity Press, 2000), Nehemiah 1:11.

WEEK 5, DAY 3: WHEN THE ENEMY ATTACKS, DO THIS

1. Andrew Knowles, *The Bible Guide* (Minneapolis: Augsburg, 2001), 203–204.

WEEK 5, DAY 4: COMPELLED TO CONTINUE, TOGETHER

1. Victor Harold Matthews, Mark W. Chavalas, and John H. Walton, *The IVP Bible Background Commentary: Old Testament* (Downers Grove, IL: InterVarsity Press, 2000), Nehemiah 6:15.

2. Mervin Breneman, *Ezra, Nehemiah, Esther,* The New American Commentary, Mervin Breneman, ed., vol. 10 (Nashville: Broadman & Holman, 1993), 213.

Bible Credits

Unless otherwise noted, all Scripture quotations are taken from the ESV® Bible (The Holy Bible, English Standard Version®), copyright © 2001 by Crossway, a publishing ministry of Good News Publishers. Used by permission. All rights reserved.

Scripture quotations marked AMP are taken from the Amplified® Bible, copyright © 2015 by The Lockman Foundation; AMPC are taken from the Amplified® Bible, copyright © 1954, 1987 by The Lockman Foundation. Used by permission. www.Lockman.org.

CEB are taken from the Common English Bible. Copyright 2012 by Common English Bible. All rights reserved.

CSB are taken from the Christian Standard Bible®, Copyright © 2017 by Holman Bible Publishers. Used by permission; HCSB are taken from the Holman Christian Standard Bible®, copyright © 1996, 2009 by Holman Bible Publishers. Used by permission. Christian Standard Bible®, CSB®, Holman Christian Standard Bible®, Holman CSB®, and HCSB® are federally registered trademarks of Holman Bible Publishers.

GNT are taken from the Good News Translation in Today's English Version—Second Edition. Copyright © 1992 by American Bible Society. Used by permission.

MSG are taken from THE MESSAGE, copyright © 1993, 2018 by Eugene H. Peterson. Used by permission of NavPress, represented by Tyndale House Publishers. All rights reserved.

Katy McCown

Speaker • Author • Podcaster

Read More
by Katy

If you were inspired by *She Belongs*, we think you'll love Katy's Bible study, *She Smiles without Fear: Proverbs 31 for Every Woman*. In this study, Katy leads you to trade your fear of the future for joy in the present and helps you find security in God's control and confidence in His plans.

KATY MCCOWN

She Smiles Without Fear

Proverbs 31 for Every Woman

To learn more about *She Smiles without Fear* and for other resources from Katy go to **www.katymccown.com**.

Connect with Katy today on social media **@katymccown**.